A
Mature Christian
Leader

Life Qualities from the Bible that define a

mature leader of God's people.

A Bible Teaching Series

Pastor James McClurg

Bundaberg, Queensland, Australia

2022

1

A Mature Christian Leader

A Bible Teaching Series by Pastor James McClurg, 2022

Acknowledgements

I wish to thank the following people who assisted by making suggestions to the content and helping to proof-read the manuscript:

Pastor Rob Booth-Jones, Senior Pastor, Mackay Christian Family Church, Queensland, Australia

Pastor Dallas Hobbs, Senior Pastor, Living Word Church, Bundaberg, Queensland, Australia

Dalme Hobbs

Sean Taggart

My wife, Anthea

I also wish to acknowledge and thank the following people, whose assistance was invaluable in completing this project.

Those from Slade Point Christian Life Centre in Mackay, Queensland, Australia, who patiently attended meetings when I first taught an earlier draft of the material in this book.

My wife, Anthea, for encouraging me along the way to complete the manuscript and publish the book, and for surrendering the many long hours that went into preparing and writing this material.

Doctor Shaun Marlow, World Harvest Ministries, Brisbane, Queensland, Australia for assistance with the process of publishing the manuscript.

Mrs Emily McClurg and Mrs Carley Nolan for book cover design, publishing design, website design and development, and assistance with publishing the document.

The words of the Apostle Paul (quoted from the AMP) :

'I, the prisoner for the Lord, appeal to you to live a life worthy of the calling to which you have been called [that is, to live a life that exhibits godly character, moral courage, personal integrity, and mature behaviour - a life that expresses gratitude to God for your salvation],' **(Ephesians 4:1)**

'The things [the doctrine, the precepts, the admonitions, the sum of my ministry] which you have heard me teach[1] in the presence of many witnesses, entrust [as a treasure] to reliable and faithful men who will also be capable and qualified to teach others.' **(II Timothy 2:2)**

'For the [remarkable, undeserved] grace of God that brings salvation has appeared to all men. It teaches us to reject ungodliness and worldly (immoral) desires, and to live sensible, upright, and godly lives [lives with a purpose that reflect spiritual maturity] in this present age,' **(Titus 2:11, 12)**

'But solid food is for the [spiritually] mature, whose senses are trained by practice to distinguish between what is morally good and what is evil.' **(Hebrews 5:14)**

---

1 - Lit through, footnote in AMP Bible text

Foreword

Pastor James McClurg has written a very thorough and thought-provoking study of the letters of Paul to Timothy and Titus, which I commend to any man or woman aspiring to a leadership position in the Kingdom of God.

It has been said that leaders are born with the ability to lead and are not made. However, I see in scripture that Jesus called different kinds of people to follow Him, and He brought forth the desired leadership qualities in their life. There is no reference in scripture that these men were leaders before Jesus called and empowered them.

Any person, male or female, who aspires to lead for the Lord, can grow into that role if they are prepared to pay the cost of growth by application of the word to their life. This means allowing the work of the Holy Spirit (*II Corinthians 3:18*) to do the necessary adjustments to Christian character development, including thinking, attitude, and humility. Availability is more important than aptitude and ability.

Time and again in scripture, both Old and New Testament, God chose the foolish things (people) of the world to confound the wise (*I Corinthians 1:27*).

In the last forty-six years, I have never regretted for a second that I became a Christian, or that I gave my life to Him in service and love. My prayer for you is that you too can say that at the end of the adventure of knowing and serving God, it was totally worth it.

May you be blessed as you read, reflect, pray over, and apply the principles expounded by Pastor James in this well-written book.

Pastor Rob Booth-Jones
Senior Minister, Mackay Christian Family Church

It is a privilege to have known Pastor James McClurg for the past five years. He is a man of prayer and a teacher of scriptural principles. Many have found his teaching practicable for daily living. His experience as a senior pastor for thirty years plus, along with the many years preaching and teaching around our nation, has certainly given him the wisdom and experience to expand on the subject 'A Mature Christian Leader'.

As I read through this book, I found myself evaluating my own life afresh. Am I living up to the values of a good leader in the body of Christ ? There are a number of areas in which Pastor James gives a very balanced view. In the section 'A believer must not be given to drunkenness', I believe Pastor James makes some valid points as so many have different views depending on how you were taught from a new convert, or family upbringing.

In this book, Pastor James brings us back to what does the scripture say ? In another section of this book, we are asked the question 'Am I temperate ?' Unless you go to the scripture, most of us would not know the answer to this.

I found this teaching not to be condemning but causing a conviction to rise up to a greater accountability in the Lord. You will be blessed as you study this subject.

Pastor Dallas Hobbs,
Senior Pastor, Living Word Church, Bundaberg
Director, Connexions, Ltd, Australia

Table of Contents

Purpose of this Bible teaching series

I have been an ordained christian minister (or pastor) for more than 36 years. Over that time, I have had the privilege of meeting many wonderful christian men and women who obviously love God with all their heart and are sincere in their christian life. Many of these dear people claim to be mature or growing in their relationship with Jesus Christ. These people honestly seek to grow closer to God in their own christian lives, but often lack an understanding of how to live as a mature christian man or woman consistent with Biblical teachings.

The Bible, which I believe is our ultimate source of truth, provides what I call Life Qualities that characterise a mature man or women of God. Each life quality is discussed in detail in this book in the order they appear in the Bible. My prayer for you as you consider these life qualities is that God will challenge you, as he has challenged me, to grow towards a more mature, Godly lifestyle.

There is a short section named 'Personal Application' at the end of the discussion on each Life Quality. This section is designed to stimulate your thinking on what you have just read and allow the Holy Spirit to challenge you to become more like Him in your daily life. If you carefully read each section and seek to apply what you learn to your own life, you will be well on your way to living as a mature man or woman of God.

At the back of this book is a self-evaluation of what you have learned from this study. If you honestly answer the questions, considering what you have read regarding each Life Quality in the text, you will be able to evaluate your maturity level as a christian.

Are you still a 'babe in Christ' even though you may have been a christian for several years (or longer) ?

Yours in Christ,

Pastor James McClurg
March 2022

Introduction to A Mature Christian Leader

We live in a time when information is available on almost any subject using a computer, mobile phone, tablet or other device. Solutions to most things that trouble us, physically, mentally, or spiritually can be easily accessed. Instant formulas can be downloaded on how to cook the perfect meal to how to grow in our spiritual life or the latest teaching from any 'hot' gospel preacher. Many christians approach spiritual maturity with this same type of thinking, expecting instant results from an internet download or spiritual formula.

➤ 'You must crucify all of self (or the flesh)' some say, and then you will suddenly rise to a new level of spirituality.

➤ Some claim that 'discovering your spiritual gifts' and beginning to function in the body of Christ as God intended is the secret to growing in your spiritual life.

➤ Being 'filled with the Spirit' is the secret to a happy and victorious christian life say others.

➤ 'Abandon yourself completely to God's will' claim others, and you are guaranteed to live a carefree life now and for eternity.

➤ Along with all these ideas there are teaching books, testimonies, YouTube or other on-line videos, Bible readings and prayer formulas guaranteed to make God work for us.

All these statements sound true and spiritual and indeed can be in some part scriptural. However, these ideas often confuse new and older christians alike who try the latest and greatest teaching to become a more mature Godly person. Some christian people often spend lots of money, time, and effort in the process.

As I reflect on my own life as a christian, I can remember trying many of these formulas, usually with very disappointing results. I ended up confused, depressed, and defeated as I tried to become a more mature God-fearing man.

One thing I have discovered over the years as a pastor, is that it takes time and personal effort to grow as a mature man or woman of God. A mature Godly person never develops from an instant formula downloaded from the internet or from reading a book (or books) on leadership. It takes time to become like Jesus Christ, a process, of course, which is not complete until we are finally with Him in heaven.

I now realise there is no instant formula to becoming a mature man or woman of God.

Christian maturity is not to be judged by chronological age, or how long anyone has been a christian. A man or woman may have been a believer for many years and yet be immature or carnal. If Paul had simply said anyone could become an elder after a certain length of time, like a probation or apprenticeship as a christian, it would allow people who were still yet babes in Christ to function as elders or leaders in a local church.

True maturity has nothing to do with spiritual gifts '*God also testified to it by signs, wonders and various miracles, and by gifts of the Holy Spirit distributed according to his will.*' (*Hebrews 2:4*). The gifts of God are not based on our works, abilities, scriptural knowledge, or maturity level (*Ephesians 2:8, 9*). I believe from these verses, that anyone can function in these gifts, and function well, yet still be spiritually immature.

How do you recognize a mature christian leader (man or woman) ?

This is not a new question. Recognising who is, and who is not, called to become an elder or leader in the local church has been an important issue since New Testament days. I believe it is still important in our modern church of the 21st Century.

Many people claim to be mature in God and want to be recognised in a leadership position in lots of local churches today. No denomination seems to be exempt from such people who are truly trying to fulfil what they believe is their God-given destiny. However, not all these people are called to leadership positions. Those who fail to be accepted as leaders may become disillusioned with, or antagonistic towards, the local church.

When Timothy stayed in Ephesus to help the newly established church, he was confronted with men who wanted to be spiritual leaders (*I Timothy 1:6, 7*). Paul commended those who desired to become overseers or church leaders. *'Here is a trustworthy saying: Whoever aspires to be an overseer desires a noble task.'* (*I Timothy 3:1*). In the following verses he lists the qualifications of those who could fulfil this noble task. (*I Timothy 3:2 – 12*).

Titus was left in Crete by Paul to appoint elders in the local churches (*Titus 1:5*), and then Paul lists the qualifications of people to be appointed as elders or overseers. (*Titus 1:6 - 9*).

In his letters to Timothy and Titus, Paul provides us with qualifications for leaders to be appointed in the local church. These qualifications are based on the level of spiritual maturity of those individuals. This spiritual maturity is discernible, both by the individual as well as those he or she relates to.

The combined list of qualifications from these two passages in *I Timothy* and *Titus* provide what I call 'Life Qualities' or spiritual qualifications that define a mature christian leader. Paul gives us this list of life qualities by bringing together many characteristics of spiritual maturity that are scattered elsewhere throughout the New Testament. There are 21 life qualities in this list, which is presented on the next page. Each of these life qualities is discussed in detail in this book.

Paul teaches us that the person who desires to be a spiritual leader must make sure he or she has developed the life qualities specified in *I Timothy chapter 3* and *Titus chapter 1*.

These life qualities apply equally to men or women. In the time and culture Paul was writing to Timothy and Titus, it was only acceptable for men to be in positions of leadership. However, in today's western society it is culturally acceptable that men or women are in leadership positions in politics, business and many religious institutions and churches.

The same Greek word, *'tis'*, is translated into the English word *'whoever'* in *I Timothy 3:1* and *'an elder'* in *Titus 1:6*. In both references, *'tis'* has a literally English meaning of *'a certain one'*[2]. There is no indication that it is referring to a man or woman in the context of these verses.

Throughout this book when referring to 'man' or 'men' I refer to man as 'mankind', not excluding women, but including women. The only exceptions are parts of the discussion of Life Quality Number 2 – 'Faithful to his wife' and 12 – 'Manage his own family well'.

---

2 - *Greek word and meaning from Strong's Concordance*

16

The 21 Life Qualities of a Mature Christian Leader are :

1. Above reproach
2. Faithful to his wife
3. Temperate
4. Selfcontrolled
5. Respectable
6. Hospitable
7. Able to teach
8. Not given to drunkenness
9. Not violent but gentle
10. Not quarrelsome
11. Not a lover of money
12. Manage his own family well
13. Not a new convert
14. A good reputation with outsiders
15. Not pursuing dishonest gain
16. Must keep hold of the deep truths of the faith with a clear conscience
17. Not overbearing
18. Must love what is good
19. Upright
20. Holy
21. Disciplined

These are more than generalisations. They are specific life qualities that are expected of every mature Godly leader. They characterise a person who has become mature in God through a long, often hard process of spiritual growth and development. Such a person has learned to reflect Jesus Christ in their total lifestyle, even when others are not watching.

Notice that in this entire list there is no reference to spiritual gifts. Paul did not say look for someone with the gift of pastor-teacher, or the gift of administration, or the gift of helps, or those who were known as encouragers. Nor did he say look for those who have a great 'platform personality' when preaching, or who are faithful in attending all the church meetings, or someone who agrees with all the pastor's or leader's vision.

There is little reference to any natural ability or skill in this list. A person's natural charisma is not included, although God can use such an ability or skill in a person when it is submissive and in tune with God's overall plan. Nor is there mention of a person's physical appearance, natural strength, position in society (status of his earthly or worldly job or family heritage) or financial resources.

Out of the twenty-one life qualities listed, nineteen are about a person's reputation, ethics, morality, temperament, habits, and spiritual and psychological maturity. One is about a man's ability to lead his own family. The other is about understanding faith and sound doctrine to be able to encourage with God's grace those who believe, and gently oppose those who refuse to believe.

I believe Paul's letters imply that a mature christian person has abandoned those attitudes and behavioural patterns that were naturally part of their former lifestyle and changed them to become Christlike. (Read for example *Ephesians 4:17 - 32*).

A mature person must have a lifestyle that is '*worthy of the Lord and please(ing) him in every way: bearing fruit in every good work, growing in the knowledge of God,*' (*Colossians 1:10*).

This is a lifestyle developed by specific decisions of someone's own self-will, combined with a conscious effort to change his or her ways, actions and reactions in their daily lives. It is only achieved by hard work and learning, usually from many failures along the way and never solely by our own strength, ability, or desire. Anyone who strives to develop and grow in this lifestyle must rely on the Holy Spirit and God's grace, for we can achieve nothing in this life without God's strength (*Ephesians 2:8, 9*).

Why these life qualities ?

These life qualities are written in the Bible concerning leaders who are to function in the local church. Therefore, these should be requirements for spiritual leaders today.

I am concerned that in many churches today, leaders are often appointed on their physical and so-called spiritual or preaching abilities, or their financial resources, or worldly connections, rather than on their level of maturity as judged against these life qualities listed in God's Word.

Anyone who has the life qualities outlined in this list can quickly develop other skills and use them for the glory of God. However, if someone becomes a spiritual leader in the local church who has lots of skill but is lacking in these life qualities, I believe they have the potential to lead people in the wrong direction.

'Where do I begin ?' you ask.

The answer is to study each of these life qualities and make them a goal for your life. Then proceed to make these life qualities part of your daily life as best you possibly can. With God's help, you can grow in your maturity level if you apply what you learn in this Bible teaching series to your daily lifestyle.

Are you up for the challenge in your daily christian life ?

Life Quality Number 1 -
Above Reproach

'*Now an overseer is to be **above reproach**'* (*I Timothy 3:2*) or *'an elder or overseer must be **blameless**'* (*Titus 1:6, 7*).

The Greek word, '*anepileeptos*' translated as '*above reproach*' in *I Timothy 3:2*, has a literal English meaning of '*that cannot be reprehended; not open to censure; irreproachable*'. The literal English meaning of the Greek word '*anegkletos*' translated as '*blameless*' in *Titus 1:6*, is '*that cannot be called to account, unreproveable, unaccused, blameless*'[3].

Combining these two Greek words and their English meanings from *I Timothy* and *Titus* indicates the English phrase '*above reproach*' refers to the day-to-day life of a christian person, such as being honest, truthful, and trustworthy. Such a person is not prone to accusations of false dealings, lying or cheating in their business or personal life. A mature Godly person who is above reproach also has a good reputation. (We will discuss the reputation with those outside the church later – when we discuss life quality 14.)

This Life Quality is placed first in the list for a reason.

It is the basis of all that follows.

---

3 - Both Greek words and English meanings from Strong's Concordance

Recognizing someone who is above reproach

How do you recognise a person who is above reproach or has a good reputation ? They have the following character traits :

- ❑ They are honest - I'd trust them with my bank account
- ❑ They keep their word (regardless of their own personal cost)
- ❑ They love people and are easy to talk to
- ❑ They don't judge or 'put down' others no matter their race or social standing
- ❑ They don't make assessments of people based on other people's opinions or rumours
- ❑ They are humble
- ❑ They are not self-centred or conceited
- ❑ They won't let you down
- ❑ They won't take advantage of you
- ❑ They are not an opportunist
- ❑ They don't use people for their own ends or to work up the promotional ladder
- ❑ They make you feel comfortable no matter who you are
- ❑ They are fair
- ❑ They don't lose their cool too easily
- ❑ They are consistent – their words match their daily lifestyle
- ❑ They recognise and respect authority
- ❑ They admit when they are wrong
- ❑ They are teachable
- ❑ You know what they are thinking
- ❑ They can keep a confidence

The concept of church leaders being above reproach is also found in the book of Acts. When the church faced its first organisational problem in Jerusalem, the apostles suggested that seven men '*with good reputations [men of godly character and moral integrity], full of the Spirit and of wisdom,*' be selected to help solve the problem of food distribution (*Acts 6:3*, AMP).

Paul heard about a man called Timothy when he came to Lystra on his second missionary journey. '*The believers at Lystra and Iconium spoke well of him.*' (*Acts 16:2*). In other words, he had a good reputation from living a life that was above reproach. Paul was impressed with Timothy's reputation; this was the man he wanted to join with him on the missionary journey (*Acts 16:3*). Notice three things about Timothy from verse 2 :

1)   People were talking about Timothy. A good reputation usually results in others talking about you in a positive rather than a negative way.

2)   More than one person was doing the talking. All of us have one or two prejudiced friends. However, the true test is what people in general are saying about you.

3)   People were talking about him in both Lystra and Iconium, that is, in more than one location. You may have a good reputation with people at your church, but what is your reputation with your neighbours, your work colleagues, friends, or family ?

It takes time to live a life that is above reproach and to build a good reputation

When a person is growing and maturing in his christian life, he or she should be developing a good reputation. The christian with a poor reputation is likely to be exhibiting life-style traits that are not in harmony with christian principles or with people's expectations of behaviour from mature personalities.

It is easy to destroy your reputation by a single, foolish act. How many good people do you know who are remembered not for all the good they have done, but for one or two mistakes that have ruined their reputation ? Many people only ever hear of the accusations of wrongdoing by a politician, teacher, or religious leader (no matter if these accusations are true or not) rather than all the good these same people have done in or for the community.

The devil will do all that he can to drag dirt up on your reputation or twist something you have said or done to try to destroy your reputation. His goal is for you to be criticised, either justly or unjustly, which is one of his best weapons against you. The devil tried to do this to Jesus on many occasions, and I am sure you can find some as read through the gospels.

Paul wrote, '*Join together in following my example...*'
(*Philippians 3:17*).

Could you say that to others ?

24

Personal application

This personal application is designed to help you begin this Bible teaching series and develop a good reputation.

Review the character traits listed of a person who is above reproach. How do you think you measure up ? The following questions may help you in this regard :

> Do I get positive feedback from those closest to me indicating I have a good reputation (such as my partner or my friends) ? Are my children glad to be known as my offspring or do they hide from this in shame ? Feedback from those who do not know you very well is generally not the best test. Their judgments can be very superficial. They may be impressed with your physical appearance, with your speaking ability, or with your 'platform' personality, which may or may not represent who you really are as a person.

> Do my relationships with people grow deeper the longer they know me and the closer they get to me, or do my friendships tend to become strained as people learn what I'm really like ?

> Do I have a reputation for not following through on commitments I have made to other people ?

> Do people trust me with confidential information ?

> Do people recommend me for significant or difficult tasks without fear that I will let them down ?

If you have difficulties in being objective about answering these questions, spend time with a close friend or your spouse and ask her/him to honestly help you evaluate your answers.

You may find answering these questions threatening, but remember it is your fear of what you might find out about yourself that may lead you to react negatively.

Maybe you already know your failings in this area and are afraid to make a change in your lifestyle. If this applies to you, I encourage you to begin to make the required lifestyle changes, so that you will be on your way to becoming a more mature Godly person.

Life Quality Number 2 -
Faithful to his wife

'*Now an overseer is to be above reproach, **faithful to his wife***'
(*I Timothy 3:2* and *Titus 1:6*)

The Greek phrase '*aner (or andra) mias gynaikos*' translated as
'*faithful to his wife*' , has a literal English meaning of '*any male person,
one, a woman, wife, my lady*'[4] . This Greek phrase is translated as '*the
husband of one wife*' in many Bible versions, such as the AMP and NKJV,
'*faithful to his wife*' (versions such as NIV) and '*faithful to their partner*'
(The Source Bible).

Many Bible commentaries and christian people argue that this
life quality is to be taken literally – the husband of one wife only with no
option for divorce or remarriage, even after the death of a spouse. Other
commentaries and christian people argue that divorce and remarriage should
be allowed for church leaders under certain or limited circumstances, such
as unfaithfulness or backsliding of the wife or her death.

Bible commentaries, such as the Guthrie *et al* (1976) and Barnes' Notes
on the Bible, suggest '*married only once*' seems more likely as the correct
English translation of this Greek phrase. Polygamy was common in the Roman
society at the time of Paul's writing, and the implication from these words is that
a christian leader should not be a polygamist. Barnes' Notes also point out that
sexual immorality was common at that time, and it was culturally acceptable
for men to be unfaithful. Hebrews teaches us that God will judge the sexually
immoral (*Hebrews 13:4*). Therefore, the requirement for a christian leader in
the church to be 'faithful to his wife' is to contrast the morality of the leader
with the acceptable morality of the society of the day.

---

4 - *Both Greek words and English meanings from Strong's Concordance*

After the death of the first wife, marrying a second wife is not condemned in scripture. Paul writes that a woman whose husband dies is free to remarry (*I Corinthians 7:39*). It is logical to infer that it is equally lawful and proper for a man to remarry after the death of his spouse. In *I Corinthians 7:12 – 16*, Paul mentions the situation where a believer has an unbelieving partner (husband or wife). '*But if the unbelieving partner leaves, let him leave. In such cases the [remaining] brother or sister is not [spiritually or morally] bound. But God has called us to peace.*' (*I Corinthians 7:15*, AMP).

God does not exclude anyone – He is always fair and just. How can we say that God excludes someone, especially when the issue may not be their fault – such as the death or adultery of a partner, or a partner choosing not to join them in following Christ ? (*Matthew 5:31, 32 ; I Corinthians 7:1 – 17*).

Therefore, I believe this life quality is about the moral purity of a christian leader rather than the issue of divorce or remarriage. It does not mean a single or divorced person is excluded from the role of church leader or from becoming mature in God (especially if this happened before someone became a christian) or infer that a single or divorced person has any more or any less problems than a married one.

> This Life Quality is about moral purity, rather than the issue of divorce or remarriage.

The issue of christian moral purity involves more than the physical act of sexual intercourse. Jesus Christ Himself spoke directly to this issue in the sermon on the mount. '*You have heard that it was said, 'You shall not commit adultery.' But I say to you that everyone who looks at a woman lustfully has already committed adultery with her in his heart*' (*Matthew 5:27, 28*).

The intent of the English word '*lustfully*' in verse 28 has a deeper meaning in the Greek than in English[5]. It is not referring to a passing glance or the momentary impulse of desire, but the continued gaze by which the impulse is deliberately allowed to continue until it becomes a passion. Our Lord's words speak primarily of adultery, but are, of course, applicable to any form of sensual impurity.

Every man (or woman), married or single, is tempted in the area of moral purity. No one can avoid completely the twenty-first century sexual temptations from magazines, movies, television commercials or some television shows. Just go down to the local newsagent, DVD store, service station or corner shop, or click onto many internet sites, and you will see pornography displayed for all to see. Add to this the multitude of scantily dressed women, especially if you happen to go to the beach or look at the so-called cheer girls at most sporting event these days, and it is not difficult to understand why many people are tempted every day of their lives.

To be tempted is **not** to sin. However, temptation **can** lead to sin. Any person who secretly and deliberately enjoys an illegitimate sexual relationship with someone of the opposite sex in their mind has, in God's sight, already committed an immoral act. There is a fine line here, of course, which is not easy to describe for every individual.

Every christian person must come to grips with his or her own inner struggles and concerns regarding moral purity. It is much better in my view to be too careful than to allow the subtle influence of the world to lead to mental adultery. Some people can handle more provocative situations without too much difficulty. Others are extremely vulnerable to any circumstance that is sexually stimulating. Sometimes to be alone can be all that is needed for temptation to lead to sin. That is why in my view men should avoid counselling or praying with women or women with men when no one else is present, as temptation can very easily turn to lust and sin either mentally or physically.

---

5 - *Elliot's Commentary*

In the provocative society in which we live and no matter what our spiritual maturity, we must guard against deliberately exposing ourselves to literature, movies, television shows, and activities of any kind designed to illegitimately excite and stimulate our sexual nature. We must guard what goes into our spirits in terms of what we see, what we listen to, and what we deliberately look at (*Matthew 6:22, 23*).

A mature christian should avoid sexual temptation. This is not to imply that it is impossible to look at pornography without sinning, but there are few men or women who, if honest, will admit they are not affected negatively by the exposure. There are some people who absolutely cannot do it without sinning. Reading the latest pornographic magazines will leave a deposit of carbon on your spiritual soul that can only be cleaned by the Word and the Spirit of God.

Some practical suggestions

We must develop good communications between husbands and wives. A married man or woman who is able to overcome most sexually stimulating situations that arise in our 21st century western society must be one who has a satisfactory sex life within the marital union.

Paul writes about this problem in *I Corinthians 7:1 - 5*. In these verses, Paul instructs both wives and husbands to meet each other's sexual needs so that satan does not lead one or the other into sexual immorality or unfaithfulness.

Paul's advice to young Timothy, who lived in a very provocative society, is still relevant today. '*Run away from youthful lusts - pursue righteousness, faith, love, and peace with those [believers]who call on the Lord out of a pure heart.*' (*II Timothy 2:22, AMP*).

We should fortify ourselves through regular study of the Word of God and prayer. Nothing dulls a desire for communication with God and the study of His Word so much as indiscriminate exposure to illegitimate sexual stimuli, and nothing is so effective in combating temptation and lust as an effective prayer life and Bible study program.

Unnecessary idleness must be avoided. This was King David's moral downfall! His temptation turned to lust and sin while he was busy doing nothing (*II Samuel chapter 11*). When temptation is strong, idleness is pure folly. It has been the downfall of many men and women, even spiritual leaders.

Honest communication in the marriage union is the key to overcoming sexual temptation. If you need help in this area of communication with your spouse, the personal application section at the end of this discussion may be helpful.

If there is a lack of understanding, sensitivity, or communication in your married life, perhaps you need someone else to help you. If you as a single or divorced person, are fighting a losing battle with lust, you need an understanding friend, helper, or prayer partner. You should seek help from someone you can trust if the problem seems beyond your control.

Please, do not share your problems with a single or married person of the opposite sex. You may need a mature Godly person who is the same sex to help you work through your problems or you may need professional christian help in this area or your life.

Personal application

The following personal application is designed to help you maintain a life of moral purity.

For the Married Couple:

Have each of you read this chapter on your own. State that your purpose is to form a common basis for discussion. Discuss the chapter together using the following questions as guidelines:

➢ How do you as a woman differ from me as a man, especially in your sexual feelings, needs, and attitudes ?

➢ How do you as a man differ from me as a woman, especially in your sexual feelings, needs, and attitudes ?

➢ What can each of us do in our attitudes and behaviour to better meet each other's needs sexually ?

For the Single or Divorced Person:

List three of the greatest problems you face regarding moral purity. Be honest with yourself and don't judge yourself too harshly. Look at these problems carefully and then honestly answer the following questions:

➢ What am I doing to accentuate these problems ?

➢ What can I do on my own to solve these problems ?

➢ Can I solve all these problems alone, or do I need help from a trustworthy friend or competent christian counsellor ?

Life Quality Number 3 - Temperate

'Now an overseer is to be above reproach, faithful to his wife, temperate' (*I Timothy 3:2*).

The Greek word '*nēpháleo*' translated as '*temperate*', has a literal English meaning of '*properly, not intoxicated, free from negative influences (intoxicants); (figuratively) clear-minded; circumspect, free from life-dominating influences*'[6]. In other words, temperate people do not easily lose their physical, psychological, or spiritual perspective, or view of life, because of their feelings, emotions, or reactions to their circumstances. They remain stable and steadfast; with clear thinking no matter what circumstances may occur in their life.

> A temperate person is 'cool, calm and collected' in most situations and not easily flustered or stressed.

Temperate people do not easily lose perspective on life and realise they are only a temporary resident on this earth. Eternal values are far more important to them than material blessings or present physical needs. Many of God's people have missed out on their God-given destiny when they are more concerned with fulfilling their earthly needs, desires or wants rather than fulfilling God's plans. Esau is a biblical example when he sold his birth right for a bowl of stew (*Genesis 25:29 – 34 and 27:1 – 40 ; Hebrews 12:16, 17*).

A temperate person evaluates circumstances in the light of the teachings of God's Word. Present circumstances do not give a temperate person false security, nor do circumstances create insecurity or uncertainty about their future.

---

6 - *Greek word and meaning from Strong's Concordance*

Temperate people realise that their wealth is not to be accumulated solely for their own pleasure, but to be used for the extension of God's kingdom (*Luke 16:13 – 15*). Their career or job, if they have one, is never an end in itself, the basis of their self-esteem, or to consume their life. Temperate people know why they are here on planet earth and understand income is only to pay the bills so that they can be a witness for Jesus.

Paul teaches us in *I Thessalonians 5:8* '*since we belong to the day, let us be sober, putting on faith and love as a breastplate, and the hope of salvation as a helmet.*' The Greek word translated as the English word 'sober' in this verse is '*nḗphō*', which has a similar meaning in English to '*nēpháleo*' found in *I Timothy 3:2* [7]. *I Thessalonians 5:8* teaches us that a temperate person has the following three characteristics prominent in their life:

1)   A person of faith. Like men of old who are described in *Hebrews chapter 11*, a temperate person lives by the promises of God. Notice the faith and action of each of these men:

- By faith Abel offered a better sacrifice than Cain (*v 4*)
- By faith, Noah built an ark (*v 7*)
- By faith, Abraham obeyed and went (*v 8*)
- By faith, Abraham offered up Isaac (*v 17*)
- By faith, Isaac blessed Jacob (*v 20*)
- By faith, Moses left Egypt (*v 27*)

'*All these people were still living by faith when they died. They did not receive the things promised; they only saw them and welcomed them from a distance, admitting that they were foreigners and strangers on earth.*' (*Hebrews 11:13*).

---

7 - *Same reference as footnote 6*

A temperate person acts on (does something to demonstrate) their faith in God's promises, even though they may not understand what may happen in the coming days, weeks, or months. When the present world seems to indicate 'all is well' and peace is here, a temperate person knows that the world is headed towards ultimate destruction.

By faith, temperate people look for the second coming of Jesus Christ to deliver them from the wrath to come (*I Thessalonians 5:9*).

2)   A person of love. Paul teaches us that that love is the greatest thing - the most important of all these three personal characteristics (*I Corinthians chapter 13*). You should read this chapter again now and note that love for people should be the greatest personal characteristic of a mature Godly person.

3)   A person of hope. Hope is the reason for a temperate person's faith and attitudes towards earthly life and material possessions (*Hebrews 11:1*). Their past, present, and future perspectives are clear, sharp, and theologically correct. They are stable in life decisions and certain of a future home with God in heaven.

Our hope is laid up for us in heaven (*Colossians 1:5*). It is the '*hope of salvation*' (*I Thessalonians 5 8*) and '*the hope of eternal life, which God, who does not lie, promised before the beginning of time*' (*Titus 1:2*). Our hope '*teaches us to say "No" to ungodliness and worldly passions, and to live self-controlled, upright and godly lives in this present age, while we wait for the blessed hope - the appearing of the glory of our great God and Saviour, Jesus Christ*' (*Titus 2:12, 13*).

Temperate people have unwavering belief that God is still in control of their destiny.

- ❑ Their hope is fixed '*on the living God*' (*I Timothy 4:10*), which allows them to '*Command those who are rich in this present world not to be arrogant nor to put their hope in wealth, which is so uncertain, but to put their hope in God, who richly provides us with everything for our enjoyment.*' (*I Timothy 6:17*).

- ❑ They hold fast the confession of their hope without wavering or doubting because '*he (God) who promised is faithful*' (*Hebrews 10:23*). Their hope is set on the grace to come when Jesus Christ is revealed at His coming (*I Peter 1:13*). Moses was a temperate man who knew the uncertainty of riches, wealth and power and chose to suffer with the children of God. (*Hebrews 11:24 – 27*)

Personal application

This personal application is designed to help you develop the quality of temperance. Answer the following questions as honestly as you can.

How does your faith in God and His Word affect :

➤ Your relationships with people ?

➤ Your priorities with finances and time ?

➤ Your motivations for what you do ?

➤ Do you really believe that heaven and hell exist and those who do not know the saving love of Jesus Christ will end up in hell ? If you say you do, how is your faith revealed in your actions and motives in your daily life ?

Are you certain in your knowledge of who you are in God and His plan for your life ? If you are, do you let current circumstances dictate your feelings and moods ?

How does your life measure up to the definition of love in *I Corinthians chapter 13* ?

Are you patient ?
Are you kind ?
Are you generous ?
Are you humble ?
Are you courteous ?
Are you unselfish ?
Are you pure in your motives ?
Are you sincere ?

How does *Hebrews 12:1* apply to your life ? Do you need to lay aside anything for God ?

➢ Read biographies or watch movies of the life of great christians.

➢ Set up priority time in your day to have time with God in personal Bible study and prayer. Remember your physical body must have rest, food, and relaxation. It is easy to lose perspective when you are mentally and emotionally exhausted.

➢ What can you learn from *I Kings chapter 19*, which is the story of Elijah who lost his perspective on life after a great victory in God (which is recorded in Chapter 18) ? See what God provided for His servant before He gave him a new 'mission'.

Life Quality Number 4 - Self-controlled

'*Now an overseer is to be above reproach, faithful to his wife, temperate, **self-controlled**'* (*I Timothy 3:2* and *Titus 1:8*).

'*For by the grace given me I say to every one of you: Do not think of yourself more highly than you ought, but rather think of yourself with sober judgment, in accordance with the faith God has distributed to each of you.*' (*Romans 12:3*).

'*For the grace of God has appeared that offers salvation to all people. It teaches us to say "No" to ungodliness and worldly passions, and to live self-controlled, upright and godly lives in this present age,*' (*Titus 2:11, 12*).

In these three passages, Paul teaches us to live a self-controlled life based on Biblical teachings about God, ourselves, and relationships with other people.

How can you recognise self-controlled people ?

❑ Self-controlled people are never 'full of themselves' or their ministry, their church, or their labours for God. They are aware that without God, they can achieve nothing (*Numbers 12:3* ; *James 4: 6 – 10*). We should boast only of what Christ has done through us (*II Corinthians 10:17* ; *Jeremiah 9:23, 24*).

- Self-controlled people view their own accomplishments in the light of God's grace. They realise they are lost without Christ. All their human abilities and achievements are useless in winning any favour with God. They realise that God in His boundless love sent His Son to die for lost humanity, including them, '*while we were still sinners*' (**Romans 5:8**).

- It is sad to me when I hear or see people of God who always boast of **their** ministry or **their** gifts, as if to say that God needs them or that no other ministry or person can ever do as much for God as they do. Such an attitude is inconsistent with biblical teaching because it is proud, and God opposes proud people (*James 4:4 – 10*).

- Self-controlled people have a proper balance in life between being someone whose gifts and abilities God can use and who gives all glory and honour to Jesus Christ. The God who created the universe loves them and chooses to do His work on this earth through them. They also know that God does not need them, and they are not indispensable for God's kingdom - they can be replaced if God so chooses. Such an understanding of God's grace sends people to their knees in humble and prayerful adoration, and then enables them to rise to a new level of righteous and godly living.

- Self-controlled people recognise their own unworthiness to be called a child of God, yet stand straight, with shoulders back and head held high because God loves and uses them for His purposes despite their fears and failings. They have a well-balanced self-image. To have a correct perspective of our place in God's family does not mean we are to be withdrawn and inhibited with a lack of self-confidence.

We must recognise that all we are and have is because of God's grace - we can achieve nothing without Him. However, we must also recognise that we have both human and divine resources to do great exploits for God.

Paul could never forget God's grace in calling and redeeming him, even though he had been persecuting christian people. How could he ever think more highly of himself than he ought to think ? His attitude regarding his own human accomplishments was to '*consider it all loss for the sake of Christ*' (***Philippians 3:1 - 11***). A self-controlled person should have similar attitudes to his own earthly achievements.

When falsely accused as inferior to other so called 'super-apostles', Paul did not hesitate to proclaim his achievements to prove his right to be called an apostle. Whenever he made mention of any of his achievements, he also made sure that his motives were properly understood. His defence was never based on what he could do for God or why God needed him. He wanted people to see him as a self-controlled person, humbly acknowledging that the sufferings and victories he had in his life and ministry were only because of God's marvellous grace in his life and nothing else (***II Corinthians chapters 11 and 12***). Jesus' parable in ***Luke 17:7 - 10*** shows that we should see ourselves as simple servants carrying out our master's orders.

Paul's encouragement for Timothy is found in ***II Timothy 1:7, 8*** '*For the Spirit God gave us does not make us timid, but gives us power, love and self-discipline. So do not be ashamed of the testimony about the Lord...*'. This is good encouragement for all of us.

Personal application

If you want to live a self-controlled life, then you need to read, reread, and study the book of Proverbs. The first seven verses of Chapter 1 reveal Proverbs are in the Bible to teach you to grow in knowledge, wisdom, and self-control.

There are two main reasons why many christian people have an unbalance self-image leading to a lack of self-control. These are listed below. Carefully read the discussion to see if either of these applies to your life.

1)   An incorrect theology. The following characteristics may help you identify if your christian life includes any incorrect theology.

➤ Theological or Bible teaching which overemphasised your unworthiness or sinful nature before God. You may now feel or believe in some way that you are nothing or worthless in yourself to ever do anything for God. You may feel that you will never be anything more than a 'pew warmer' in God's house each week.

➤ You are and have been trying so hard to 'crucify your old self or the flesh' that you now believe everything in you is so bad or evil that any image of God in you is so corrupted or tainted by sin that it is now lost and unrecognisable.

➤ An incorrect view of forgiveness and being right with God so that now you are trying so hard to become nothing or 'holy' so that God can accept you.

➤ Theological or Bible teaching that to be humble before God means you should be intimated by most other christian people so that anything God has done for you or taught you is insignificant compared to what God has done for or taught everyone else.

2)   Circumstances in your past life negatively affected and may continue to affect your self-image or self-worth. These circumstances are :

> Bad experiences in school or in the neighbourhood, such as being bullied, have caused you to believe that you are always inferior to most other people.

> Bad influences from others, such as a close friend letting you down, reinforce that you are so bad that God could never love you or use you for His purposes.

> Physical illness, disability or race have created feelings of inferiority or insecurity in the sight of God when you compare yourself to other people.

Remember: You cannot do anything to become right with God but must come just as you are and accept His free gift of salvation, because He loves you. He can use you for his glory even though He knows all your past, all your faults, all your weaknesses and all your failings.

Now that you have established if you have a problem, read again the discussion above on self-controlled people. What can you learn about your unbalanced self-image or lack of self-control ? How can you apply what you learn to change your self-image ?

Ask God to help you overcome if you have a problem in any of these areas of self-control. Remember the Word of God teaches us '*If any of you lacks wisdom, you should ask God, who gives generously to all without finding fault, and it will be given to you.*' (*James 1:5*).

You may need to talk with someone you trust - someone who is a wise and trustworthy christian. Ask that person to help you develop perspective and to pray with you about your problem. Set up specific goals for your life in this area.

Some suggestions are:

➢ Being able to cope when others get the limelight or reward for something you think you deserve recognition for.

➢ Not rationalising immature behaviour because of what happened to you in the past.

➢ Becoming a responsible person, not blaming your problems on someone else, even though they may have contributed to the problem.

➢ Living so that you show you have God's love and power working through you regardless of your physical appearance, stature, race, disability, or age.

If you can honestly say before God that you don't have any problems in these areas, pray and ask God how you could help others who may have these or similar struggles.

Life Quality Number 5 - Respectable

'*Now an overseer is to be above reproach, faithful to his wife, temperate, self-controlled, **respectable**'* (**I Timothy 3:2**).

The Greek word '*kosmion*' translated as '*respectable*' in **I Timothy 3:2**, has a literal English meaning of '*orderly, virtuous, decent, modest, well-ordered*'. Paul uses a different Greek word, '*sem-nos*', translated as '*worthy of respect*' in **1 Timothy 3:8**, which has a literal English meaning of '*reverend, venerable, serious, honourable, grave, dignified, deeply respected.*'[8]

To be a respectable person is to live a well-ordered, virtuous, decent, modest, dignified, and honourable life which demonstrates Godly principles to a dying world.

The Bible has a lot to say about how we are to live our lives in a respectable manner which will not cause others to stumble in their christian life and to silence those who criticize the people of God.

Jesus said to his disciples : '*Things that cause people to stumble are bound to come, but woe to anyone through whom they come. It would be better for them to be thrown into the sea with a millstone tied around their neck than to cause one of these little ones to stumble. So watch yourselves.*' (**Luke 17:1 - 3**).

'*Therefore, let us stop passing judgement on one another. Instead, make up your mind not to put any stumbling block or obstacle in the way of a brother or a sister*' (**Romans 14:13**).

---

8 - Both Greek words and English meanings from Strong's Concordance

'*So whether you eat or drink or whatever you do, do it all for the glory of God. Do not cause anyone to stumble, whether Jews, Greeks, or the church of God - even as I try to please everyone in every way. For I am not seeking my own good but the good of many, so that they may be saved*' (***I Corinthians 10:31 - 33***).

'*Whatever happens, conduct yourselves in a manner worthy of the gospel of Christ.*' (***Philippians 1:27***)

'*Be wise in the way you act toward outsiders; make the most of every opportunity. Let your conversation be always full of grace, seasoned with salt, so that you may know how to answer everyone.*' (***Colossians 4:5, 6***).

'*Yet we urge you, brothers and sisters, to do so more and more, and to make it your ambition to lead a quiet life: You should mind your own business and work with your hands, just as we told you, so that your daily life may win the respect of outsiders and so that you will not be dependent on anybody.*' (***I Thessalonians 4:10 - 12***).

'*Live such good lives among the pagans that, though they accuse you of doing wrong, they may see your good deeds and glorify God on the day he visits us.*' (***I Peter 2:12***).

<u>A true story.</u> There were two christian women who both worked in similar positions in the same company. A more senior position became available, and they both applied for it. The one who gained the promotion lied and told a story about how bad the other 'sister' was in her work. The one who missed the promotion heard about the reason and left the church due to what this 'christian sister' had done to her.

46

<u>Another true story.</u> A christian pastor believed that God wanted him to build a school - a special school that would give a christian education to disadvantaged students. However, to build the school on the only block of land available in the price range he could afford, would break some Government regulations. He proceeded with the plan, and the matter ended up in court.

A christian friend, who worked for the Government, was called on as a witness to defend the Government regulations. The pastor chose to discredit his christian friend in the court to try to win the case and gain approval for his school.

<u>Another true story.</u> A christian minister paid little attention to the outward appearance of his home. He allowed the lawn to grow long and when he did mow it, he always left a very untidy appearance. Weeds grew rampant, and he never watered his lawn which soon became a brown 'patch' in an otherwise green and tidy street. He never had time to grow a garden, which he thought was a worldly activity that was below his spiritual calling.

Most of the neighbours paid special attention to the outward appearance of their homes, lawns and gardens and were totally turned off by this minister's lack of caring for the beauty of their street. Consequently, the neighbours were convinced that christians (ministers particularly) were a bad influence, quite lazy and unconcerned about outward beauty. There was a real barrier created to any christian witness in the area.

<u>The interpretation</u> All three stories illustrate how a man (or woman) can be a christian, or even a pastor, and not measure up to the qualification of being 'respectable'.

Paul uses the same Greek word, '*kosmion*' (translated as '*respectable*' in *I Timothy 3:2)*, when he writes women should dress '*modestly*' in *I Timothy 2:9, 10* [9] - '*I also want the women to dress modestly, with decency and propriety, adorning themselves, not with elaborate hairstyles or gold or pearls or expensive clothes, but with good deeds, appropriate for women who profess to worship God.*' He is referring in these verses to the woman who attempts to attract attention to herself - not to the Lord who she claims to serve - by means of her outward appearance. This is not calling attention to Jesus Christ, and is therefore not orderly or respectable behaviour.

A person can dress extravagantly, or be scruffy, unkempt, or even unclean. Both show a lack of respectability and draw attention to themselves rather than the Lord who they claim to serve.

Many christian women (and men), misinterpret what Paul is saying and appear drab, messy, unorganised, and untidy, thinking that such suffering and abandoning worldly pleasures somehow pleases God or shows how spiritual they are. They miss the whole point of Paul's concern, which is inner beauty and holy motives.

Christian men can also overdo 'dress to impress' to draw attention to themselves and not to the God they claim to serve. Some pastors wear designer clothes or expensive suits (men) or dresses (women) to impress others or to show how spiritually successful they are or think they are. This is also drawing attention to themselves rather than the God they claim to serve.

---

9 - Greek word and meaning from Strong's Concordance

By contrast, a person who is unattractive externally also calls attention to themselves and presents an image of Jesus Christ as one of being backward, sloppy, un-cultured, and 'peculiar' in the bad sense of that word.

> Living a respectable life has nothing to do with the price tag on the clothes or shoes you wear, the value of your house, or what type of car you drive. It is about your daily lifestyle being consistent with biblical principles.

Whether it is in your outward appearance, speech, the appearance of your home, or the way you conduct yourself with other people in the business world, or while shopping or eating out or driving your car - all are to be in proper relationship to Biblical principles. Since God is a God of order, a christian person should also be orderly, culturally proper and a gentleman or lady in all areas of their life.

Most non-christian people have a view of what is expected behaviour or dress code of those who profess to be a christian. How many times have you or I heard the phrase – 'How come you are doing that, I thought you were a christian ?' OR 'I thought so and so was a christian until he or she did ....'. There have been many, many sad stories of so and so who said he was a christian but then they did this to me.

I have counselled too many people who are now outside of the kingdom of God, but were once inside it, who became disillusioned and left because of the actions of some so-called christian person. Many times, it is a pastor or elder that they claim caused the problem. This should <u>NOT</u> be so and, where true, shows that the man or woman involved was not acting in a respectable way.

Personal application

This personal application is designed to help you develop the quality of respectability. Compare your current lifestyle against what we have discussed above. The following questions will help guide you. Answer each question as honestly as you can.

➤ Is the way I look when I leave home to go to work, church, or the shop, proper for a mature christian person both biblically and culturally ?

➤ Am I attracting attention to myself by the clothes I wear or to the Lord Jesus Christ who lives within me ?

➤ Does the house I live in impress people, or does it glorify Jesus Christ ? Size, cost, and location of your house are not important; your motives for living there are!

➤ Does my general lifestyle reflect the lifestyle of Jesus Christ ? Do I tend to draw people to Jesus Christ, or do I tend to turn them away or put them off christianity ?

How does my general speech measure up to God's standards ?

➤ Do I glorify God with my words, or do I glorify myself ?

➤ Is my speech acceptable to God and what people expect of a christian ?

Consider the scripture verses listed at the beginning of the discussion on this life quality. How does your current lifestyle compare to the principles laid out in these verses ?

From this study, isolate any areas of weakness in respectability in your own life, then set up these areas as goals for improvement. For example, if you are a person who enjoys the scruffy and unkempt look when you leave home every day, make a new goal to be well-groomed and well-dressed every day for a whole week. Concentrate on this goal until you have developed a new habit.

Only you can put actions into your life to achieve your goals. Bad habits are hard to break, but you must break them if you are to become respectable and strive to become more and more like Jesus Christ in your daily life.

Life Quality Number 6 - Hospitable

'*Now an overseer is to be above reproach, faithful to his wife, temperate, self-controlled, respectable, **hospitable**' (I Timothy 3:2 and Titus 1:8)*

Hospitality is not restricted to Christianity. It has been an important part of the lives of the people of many cultures for a long time, and even considered a sacred responsibility in some cultures. In the Old Testament, God gave specific instructions to the children of Israel regarding their duty to be hospitable to strangers.

'*When a foreigner resides among you in your land, do not mistreat them. The foreigner residing among you must be treated as your native-born. Love them as yourself, for you were foreigners in Egypt. I am the LORD your God.*' (**Leviticus 19:33, 34**).

What God instructed in the Old Testament is reconfirmed in the New and given even a greater dimension.

'*Share with the Lord's people who are in need. Practice hospitality.*' (**Romans 12:13**)

'*Keep on loving one another as brothers and sisters. Do not forget to show hospitality to strangers, for by so doing some people have shown hospitality to angels without knowing it*' (**Hebrews 13:1, 2**).

'*Above all, love each other deeply, because love covers over a multitude of sins. Offer hospitality to one another without grumbling.*' (*I Peter 4:8, 9*)

It is clear from these verses that christians are to be hospitable. Christian hospitality is to be practiced in a context of love and not a sacred responsibility or religious duty. Love provides the basic motivation for reaching out to others, and one of the best ways is to be hospitable.

Christians are to love others, not for reward, but because God first loved us (*I John 4:19*). Receiving a reward for hospitality, inviting only others who you know will invite you back, to claim a tax deduction, or asking the church to pay for it or reimburse you, should never be a part of our motive for being hospitable (*Luke 6:27 - 36* and *14:12 - 14*).

It is clear from the scriptures that christian hospitality, first, is to be demonstrated toward other believers. It is also obvious that we as christians are to be hospitable towards all men. We must love all people - regardless of race, skin colour or social standing, whether we want to or not. To do less is to violate the law of love instituted by Jesus Christ Himself.

Jesus reminds us that God's love is also the christian's bridge to the world. '*By this everyone will know that you are my disciples, if you love one another.*' (*John 13:35*).

Sound doctrine, powerful worship or prayer meetings, inspirational preaching, conferences, up to date music and technology, Bible readings, door knocking, witnessing or car bumper stickers are not mentioned by Jesus as the means to let everyone know you are His disciples. People will be drawn to know Jesus by your love (which includes hospitality).

These things, in the highlighted text box above, are important for us to do, but without our love they will never be the focus that draws people to have a personal encounter with Jesus Christ. Many people in the world do not see Christ in us because we, His church, do not show love to the people of the world as we should!

Some christian people put more of their energy into gaining position or recognition in the church than showing love and hospitality to those who are outside of the church. This should never be true of a mature christian leader.

There are times when every member of the body of Christ should join with others in showing hospitality. Don't wait for a desire to show hospitality, as the desire is not natural to most people. You will have to start showing hospitality before you begin to feel like you have a reward for your efforts.

Some hindrances to christian hospitality.

☐ Some people never invite anyone over because they think they can't afford it. You could start by inviting someone over for a simple 'cuppa. By NOT being hospitable with what you do have now, you may be robbing yourself by not allowing God to bless you and provide for your needs.

☐ Other people may feel their house is not good enough to invite someone over for a visit. So what if you do not have the flashiest house in town! Remember - the motive is christian love. The people invited are not there to give you a house inspection.

☐ If you are shy and reserved, waiting for an invitation, and then criticising others for being unfriendly, reach out to others, even though you are afraid. You will be surprised how quickly others will respond to you. It will be in giving that you will begin to receive. *Proverbs 18:24* '*A man who has friends must himself be friendly*' (NKJV).

□ Being hospitable may threaten you. Remember *'There is no fear in love. But perfect love drives out fear'* (*I John 4:18*). As you begin to practice biblical love and hospitality, fear will subside.

Some practical suggestions to help you to be hospitable :

□ Look for opportunities to share your home with spiritual leaders - pastors, missionaries, and other christian workers. Invite them to dinner or to stay in your home.

□ Look for opportunities to share your home with other members of the body of christ from your own local church. There doesn't have to be any special physical need to show hospitality. Perhaps the need is social and emotional and spiritual.

□ Many christians are lonely and in need of fellowship but may be too shy to reach out to others. They are waiting for an invitation to share their lives with someone else.

□ Begin to show hospitality to non-christians by starting with the people all around you - your neighbour across the street, or the person who works beside you at your job.

□ You are the christian; you are the one who should be reaching out to them. Invite them to dinner or ask them to join you in an evening of relaxation and social activity (no-one can resist a good BBQ).

Being hospitable may begin with having coffee at a local coffee shop. I have coffee or a 'cuppa' with many of my work and church friends and discount or loyalty cards for almost every coffee place in town.

Don't get overly ambitious.

Start by building deep friendships with one or two non-christians. Frequently this sets the stage for an invitation to a Bible Class in your home, or a personal witness for Christ.

To invite non-christians to a Bible study means building friendships first. You must learn to love people because Christ first loved you and not just because you want to win them to Christ.

Personal application

This personal application is designed to help you develop the quality of hospitality.

You must come to grips with that which is basic to any hospitality - love. Restudy the profile of biblical love in *I Corinthians 13:4 - 7*. Do you really love others ?

Honestly review the hindrances to hospitality mentioned above. Do any of these apply to you or your family ? If so, what steps can you take to overcome the problem ?

Review the practical suggestions listed above. Decide on some specific ways to show hospitality - first to members of the body of Christ, and second to those outside of the church.

Now that you have an overview, set up some specific hospitality goals.

Life Quality Number 7 -
Able to teach

'*Now an overseer is to be above reproach, faithful to his wife, temperate, self-controlled, respectable, hospitable, **able to teach**' (**I Timothy 3:2**)*

Titus 1:9 an elder (or overseer) '*..must hold firmly to the trustworthy message as it has been taught, so that he can encourage others by sound doctrine and refute those who oppose it.*'

'*The things [the doctrine, the precepts, the admonitions, the sum of my ministry] which you have heard me teach[10] in the presence of many witnesses, entrust [as a treasure] to reliable and faithful men who will also be capable and qualified to teach others.*' (***II Timothy 2:2,*** AMP)

Most people can think of 'good teachers' - people who are effective communicators, able to use skilful methods and motivate people to learn. We may think of high - powered lecturers, individuals who can hold an audience spellbound for an hour or more with ability and skill. Some of us may remember excellent teachers from our school days. We may even think of a pastor or evangelist who can hold the audience in the edge of their seats with a wonderful delivery of a sermon.

However, these instances or people are not what Paul had in mind when he wrote to Timothy in this verse. Paul is not to referring to the 'gift of teaching', as one of the gifts of the Holy Spirit (***Romans 12:7***). The New Testament teaches that this gift is given to only certain people (***Ephesians 4:11 ; I Corinthians 12:28, 29***), but being 'able to teach' is a life quality that every christian man and woman can and must develop to be mature.

---

10 - Lit through, footnote in AMP Bible text

To be 'able to teach' is essential for being a parent, as well as a functioning member of the body of Christ. Parents are to teach their children (*Ephesians 6:4*), and all members of the body of Christ are to teach and admonish one another (*Colossians 3:16*).

Paul uses the Greek word, '*didaktikon*', translated into the English phrase 'able to teach' in *I Timothy 3:2* and in *II Timothy 2:24 - 26* [11] '*And the Lord's servant must not be quarrelsome but must be kind to everyone, able to teach, not resentful. Opponents must be gently instructed, in the hope that God will grant them repentance leading them to a knowledge of the truth, and that they will come to their senses and escape from the trap of the devil, who has taken them captive to do his will.*' (Emphasis added to the Biblical text).

Paul was instructing Timothy that anyone who is 'able to teach' must be able to communicate with others in a non-threatening and gentle manner, which is similar to his words in *Titus 1:9*. When verbally, or even physically, attacked, a mature christian person does not respond with cutting words and 'put downs', 'play the person', seek revenge or become argumentative. Instead, a mature christian person should respond with grace, love and respect for the other person, or in some cases people, even though he or she doesn't agree with what the other person is (or people are) saying. The goal is to respond with God's love, hoping that the opposing person (or people) will be set free from the Devil's trap by finding the truth of God's Word for themselves.

A man or woman who is 'able to teach' is someone who holds firmly regarding the truth of God's Word and can communicate this to others, even those who oppose Biblical truth

---

11 - Greek word and meaning from Strong's Concordance

A person who is able to teach must uphold the Word of God as the final authority on any subject and understand the scriptures sufficiently to be able to encourage others in sound doctrine and gently refute those who contradict. You or I cannot communicate effectively what we don't know, and we can't know the Word of God unless we actively study it. As maturing christians, therefore, we must continue to learn more of God's Word and understand it. '*Do your best to present yourself to God as one approved, a worker who does not need to be ashamed and who correctly handles the word of truth*' (**II Timothy 2:15**).

A good knowledge and understanding of scripture and doctrine will not automatically solve your personality problems. Many people who know the Bible from cover to cover are defensive and highly threatened people, frequently using the scriptures as a 'personal' sword rather than the 'sword of the Spirit'. They often have serious problems in communicating God's Word in a non-threating manner. Such people are not mature enough to be christian leaders.

Some practical suggestions

- Undertake a Bible correspondence course or class or become involved in a Bible study group in your church where you can participate by asking questions and if you can, help lead the study.

- If people attack you personally, never retaliate. Respond warmly and with openness. If you are too emotional at that moment to respond objectively, it is better to refrain from commenting until you have developed a degree of objectivity and are in control of your emotions. '*A gentle answer turns away wrath, but a harsh word stirs up anger*' (**Proverbs 15:1**).

❑ Never retaliate publicly, especially from the pulpit, which could destroy your reputation. Many people may not see the initial attack on you first, but they will see any public attack from you. Seek to speak to those who have wronged you in a private setting. This is even true when disciplining your children. This may not always be possible or even advisable, but it is usually a good principle to follow.

❑ If you continue to have problems with insecurity or threatened feelings when you try to speak to people, seek out a mature christian friend or counsellor for helpful advice. Try to understand the reasons for your problem and be open and honest about the situation and how you may overcome these feelings.

❑ Don't give up when you fail. Learn from the failure, and next time you are likely to succeed. The more you succeed, the more confidence you will develop. God does not care how many times you fail – but he does care if you don't get up and try again.

Personal application

The following personal application is designed to help you develop the quality of being 'able to teach'.

- ➤ Develop a regular program of Bible study - either personally or in a group or both. This should be more than devotional study, but serious Bible study, designed to learn the basic content and doctrines of the Bible as well as more 'in-depth' material. Your Bible study should be personal – not just learning from books, videos, or courses, or the time spent preparing sermons or lessons for church activities.

- ➤ You cannot live and grow physically on a diet solely of second hand or junk food; nor can you live and grow spiritually on second-hand revelations.

- ➤ Devotional books, Bible study courses, on-line or by correspondence or attending classes, may be helpful. There are also Bible study aids, such as a Bible dictionary, concordance, commentary, or atlas, available through Bible apps on your phone or computer. Many of these are free or with a small annual subscription. You should be using these, where available, in your personal study.

- ➤ I believe some memorization of Bible verses and where to find them quickly is also extremely important. A good help for those who have a hard time remembering or memorizing is to have verses or short notes in the front of your Bible or tucked away inside your mobile phone cover.

> Begin to develop your personality to be non-threatened when discussing the Word of God and related subjects with all types of people. Remember it is *NOT* your job to convert anyone, leave that up to the Holy Spirit (*John 16 :7 – 11*).

> Review the practical suggestions above. How can these be applied to your life ?

Life Quality Number 8 -
Not given to drunkenness

'not given to drunkenness' (*I Timothy 3:3 and Titus 1:7*)

In New Testament days, wine was a common drink, as it is in many other cultures today. Furthermore, the degree of alcoholic content varied. If Paul were living in our Australian culture today, what would he say about drinking alcoholic beverages ?

In *I Timothy* and *Titus* Paul did not mention total abstinence from any form of alcoholic beverage. The Greek phrase, *'me paroinon'*, in these verses has a literal English meaning of *'someone who sits too long at his wine'*[12]. In other words, someone who overdrinks, gets drunk and may be even addicted to alcohol. Such a person has a reputation for having a 'hangover' and often regrets their actions or what they said after they sober up.

A mature Christian person is not to be 'given to drunkenness'. Paul was very definite on this matter, both in his letter to Timothy and to Titus. He did not say they could not partake of wine; but do not to be addicted to it or have a reputation for drinking too much.

> Both the Old and New Testament instruct us in no uncertain terms regarding drunkenness. It is out of order for a mature christian !

The scriptures make it clear that no drunkard will inherit the kingdom of God (*I Corinthians 6:9 – 11 ; Ephesians 5:18* and *I Peter 4:2, 3*). There is also a warning in scripture not to associate with a 'brother' who is a drunkard (*I Corinthians 5:11* and *Proverbs 23:29 - 35*).

---

12 - *The Lockman Foundation (1981)*

What about Paul's instruction to Timothy in *I Timothy 5:23* ? '*Stop drinking only water, and use a little wine because of your stomach and your frequent illnesses.*' The Greek word, '*oino*', translated as the English word 'wine' in this verse, is unclear whether it refers to fermented (alcoholic wine) or non-fermented grape juice[13].

Though Paul instructed Timothy to use a little for health reasons, he also taught the Romans in *Romans 14:21* '*It is better not to eat meat or drink wine or to do anything else that will cause your brother or sister to fall.*' (Read *verses 14 - 23* to understand the full context of this verse). Paul writes similar instructions to the church in Corinth (*I Corinthians 8:9 – 13*).

The problem Paul was referring to in *Romans 14* and *I Corinthians 8* was more than simply eating the meat or drinking the wine. It was the idolatrous associations of the meat and wine, and the problems partaking may create for other christians. There are times, Paul was saying, that total abstinence is the better way to live.

Love for others is a higher principle to follow when determining what is right or wrong for a christian to do or be involved in, and a mature, sensitive christian is willing to avoid certain activities, even if they may be OK in themselves.

We have two direct teachings from the Word of God regarding alcoholic drink :

1. To be addicted to it is a mark of christian immaturity and anyone with a reputation for over drinking or being drunk is not in my view honouring the God they say they serve.
2. There are times and situations when total abstinence is the best way to live. To partake may cause another christian to stumble or sin against God. Every mature christian must be cautious to follow this higher principle whenever it is necessary.

13 - Thayer (1979)

I believe because of the second teaching from the Word of God that we in Australia should **NOT** partake of **any** alcoholic drink in public. The reason is because of the major problems that alcohol causes in our society. Most non-christian people expect christian people not to drink alcohol; I believe because they know the associated evil it causes. How can we help those who are, or have been, affected by drink either directly or indirectly, if we partake ourselves, have the same reputation as them, or a fridge regularly stocked with alcohol ?

Let me go a step further.

Paul makes no specific mention of other forms of indulgence in *I Timothy chapter 3* and *Titus chapter 1*. However, the Bible is clear that to allow yourself to be controlled by **anything** is sin.

'"I have the right to do anything," you say - but not everything is beneficial. "I have the right to do anything"—but I will not be mastered by anything.' (*I Corinthians 6:12*)

'For we know that our old self was crucified with him so that the body ruled by sin might be done away with[14], that we should no longer be slaves to sin because anyone who has died has been set free from sin' (*Romans 6:6, 7*)

'For sin will no longer be a master over you, since you are not under Law [as slaves], but under [unmerited] grace [as recipients of God's favor and mercy]' (*Romans 6:14*, AMP).

---

14 - 'or be rendered powerless', footnote from text of the NIV Bible

67

'So whether you eat or drink or whatever you do, do it all for the glory of God. Do not cause anyone to stumble, whether Jews, Greeks or the church of God - even as I try to please everyone in every way. For I am not seeking my own good but the good of many, so that they may be saved.' (**I Corinthians 10:31 - 33**).

'For a man is the slave of whatever masters him' (**II Peter 2:19**, JB PHILLIPS).

A mature christian does nothing that deliberately harms their body or makes themselves an ineffective instrument for Christ (**I Corinthians 6:19, 20**). Are you overindulging in any of these in your life ?

- ❑ Soapies or certain other T.V. shows or movies (e.g., regular nudity, lust, immorality, or cursing Jesus' name)

- ❑ Obsessive desire for more worldly wealth

- ❑ Gambling - such as horse races, lotto, casket, scratchies or power ball

- ❑ Work – being a workaholic who wants to succeed in the business world no matter what the cost

- ❑ Nicotine - smoking

- ❑ Sport - particularly football, cricket and the olympic or commonwealth games

- ❑ Addiction to the latest movies, newest computers, the internet, or computer games

❑ Obsessive desire for the 'body beautiful', e.g., overuse of exercise programs, plastic surgery, or diets.

There may be nothing wrong with most of the things mentioned above, in themselves. However, I believe any of these things listed above is sin when:

1) It causes another christian to stumble and sin

2) It becomes an addiction in your life that is not doing you any physical or emotional good

3) It is stealing quality time with your family and/or God

4) It robs you of money or time that you could otherwise give to God's work

The devil comes to steal, kill, and destroy (*John 10:10*). Therefore anything that steals or robs you of something comes from him, especially if it robs you of time with God. So many christians justify themselves in these areas. I am cutting down on this, slowly, or I am doing much better than I used to. I believe that the Bible is clear – you are to get rid of it completely. *You are much better off without it*.

Read and remind yourself of *Hebrews 12:1*. It is time to get rid of the things that so easily entangle you (even though they may not necessarily be sinful in themselves).

Are you judging your brother who is taking a christian liberty you do not take ? If you are, you may be violating a commandment of God (*Romans 14:3, 5*).

There are only two biblical justifications for any christian criticising or judging a brother who takes a liberty in an area you do not. These are:

1) He or she is over-indulging and hurting himself and/or his testimony.

2) He or she is causing other christians to stumble and sin.

Personal application

The following personal application is designed to help you develop a lifestyle consistent with Biblical principles.

Examine your own attitudes to the indulgences listed above. You may consider yourself a mature christian having developed certain boundaries for your own life. In doing so, are there any areas in your life that are causing other christians to stumble and fall or sin, even though they may be quite OK for you ?

What do you do as a christian that harms your body or clouds your thinking, or brings you into bondage to yourself ?

Remember: A mature christian faces his problems and solves them. The following specific suggestions may help you :

➢ Isolate the problem. Write out the problem on a piece of paper and set out a specific goal that you wish to accomplish in overcoming the problem. Read your goal several times a day if necessary.

➢ Discuss it with other mature christians if need be or if appropriate. If they concur that it is a real problem, ask them to pray regularly for you.

➢ Develop a regular time to study the scriptures, and to meditate and pray about the problem.

➢ Many christian people have found that a period of fasting and praying has helped them break habits that are dominating or sinful.

➤ If you cannot overcome your problem through personal encounter with God and through the prayers of other members of the body of Christ, then seek help from a competent christian counsellor. Your problem may have hidden or deeper causes that you need to understand and come to grips with before you can overcome the problem.

Life Quality Number 9(a) - Not violent

'*not given to drunkenness, **not violent***' (*I Timothy 3:3*)

'*Since an overseer manages God's household, he must be blameless - not overbearing, **not quick-tempered***' (*Titus 1:7*)

The Greek word, '*plekten*' translated into the English words '*violent*' or '*quick-tempered*', has a literal English meaning of '*anger out of control, not just verbally, but also physically*'[15]. The English phrases 'not violent' or 'not quick-tempered' in Paul's letters to Timothy and Titus refer to someone who strikes violently in explosive bursts of uncontrollable rage or anger against anyone or any situation that causes them to be angry. These angry outbursts can be accompanied by rage, malice, slander, and filthy language. Both English phrases immediately follow or precede '*not given to drunkenness*'. The connection, of course, is obvious. Many brawls have started where someone (or more than one person) has consumed alcohol.

Historically, physical violence against other human beings has been generally condemned, both in the laws of our land and in the minds and hearts of people. Child abuse, wife beating, anti-social behaviour against other people or police brutality against criminals generally disgust most people. **And rightly so**.

A mature Godly person is not violent - either verbally or physically, or someone who 'flies off the handle' or 'goes from calm to volcano in a very short moment'. He or she is in control, even on the rare occasions when they may be angry with proper motives.

---

15 - Thayer (1979)

Such a person refuses to allow violence to continue or 'to stoop to the other person's level' by retaliation and is always gracious and forgiving even when provoked or wronged by others.

God is displeased with physical violence. In certain circumstances God used the children of Israel themselves to judge unrighteous nations. God's command to destroy them was always because of the sin and moral collapse of these nations. The children of Israel were never commanded by God to destroy another nation or people in a rage of personal or national anger because of what that nation or people had done to them. God always disapproves of uncontrollable anger that is motivated by personal vindictiveness.

The scriptures provide us with many examples of a person who becomes violent towards someone because of uncontrolled anger. God's displeasure is obvious, even when it happens to be one of His choicest servants. Some biblical examples are:

CAIN became jealous because God favoured his brother's offering more than his. He chose not to overcome the sin in his own life (*Genesis 4:6, 7*). What that sin was we are not told. Cain allowed his anger and hatred toward Abel to grow until he eventually lost control. He murdered his brother in a fit of rage and never sought forgiveness from God. Note that God punished Cain severely only after lovingly giving him an opportunity to confess and repent of what he had done (*Genesis 4:9*). God spared his life, but Cain was plagued the rest of his days with a curse for his evil deeds (*Genesis 4:10 - 16*).

MOSES lost his position in Egypt when he failed to control his temper and slew an Egyptian for severely beating an Israelite slave (*Exodus 2:11 - 16*).

After he had received the Ten Commandments from God on the mountain, Moses saw the people engaged in idolatry. He became so angry that he threw the tablets of stone onto the ground, and they broke into pieces (*Exodus 32:19*). This was a deliberate act of throwing them down in anger rather than simply dropping them when he saw what God's people had become.

On another occasion, Moses disobeyed God by striking a rock twice to bring forth water, rather than speaking to the rock as God had commanded. Moses had allowed his anger to control him, and he was punished by God (*Numbers 20:10, 11*). God did not allow this to go uncorrected, (*Numbers 20:12*), even though it meant disciplining the man He had allowed to come into His very presence (*Exodus 33:12 – 22* and *chapter 34*).

Even though he was gentle, meek, and mild and generally in control of his emotions and human spirit, Moses still had an anger problem. It was because of this pattern of uncontrolled anger outbursts, often violent, that he missed the promised land, not just any one isolated incident.

This should serve as a warning for all of us - God does not continue to tolerate a pattern of uncontrolled violence or anger in anyone, even in His chosen leaders.

PETER took matters into his own hands. He had bragged about his courage never to forsake the Lord! To save face, when the soldiers had come to take Jesus, he drew his sword in anger at what was about to happen to Jesus and struck the servant of the High Priest, Malchus, missing his neck but cutting off his right ear. Jesus touched and healed Malchus but commanded Peter to put away his sword. Peter ran off into the night and later denied the Lord three times (*Luke 22:49 – 51* and *John 18:10, 11*).

When put under pressure and personally threatened, some people can develop other ways of getting even with someone rather than with physical violence. Verbal abuse, internet bullying and character assassination on social media in our culture are often more effective in hurting others than using physical violence. It is much easier to recover from physical bruises and even broken bones than to recover from a broken heart or a bruised spirit.

Some people develop or enjoy verbal attack against others, which is often disguised as personal concern. It sounds spiritual to share morsels of gossip in the context of prayer - to say, for example, "Don't tell anybody but....". Gossip and malicious talk, especially when disguised as spiritual concern, are the most dangerous form of violence because the true motives are hidden under a pretence of compassionate or concerned prayer. If you talk frequently about others and to a variety of people, if you tend to repeat stories about a person and enjoy doing so, chances are you are 'getting even' with someone. This is still 'violence' in God's eyes.

Notice that in *I Timothy chapter 3* or *Titus chapter 1*, Paul did not teach that all anger is sinful. Nor does he imply we are truly spiritual when we are meek and mild and let the devil, the world and everyone in it walk all over us as a doormat. Such verses as *Matthew 5:39* are used to support this argument – proclaiming that God wants us to be whimps!

This interpretation of the Bible is incorrect in my view because it takes verses such as this out of context and does not consider what the Bible teaches in other verses, such as the following:

❑ God was often angry because of the sin of His people (*Numbers 11:1* and *12:9 ; Zechariah 1:2*).

- Jesus Christ was angry with the money changers in God's temple (*Mark 11:15 – 17*). He was angry because people could not see that God could heal on the Sabbath (*Mark 3:5*). Jesus Christ was never vindictive in his anger or displayed any hint of getting even. His anger was controlled by God's love.

We all can also express feelings of love and anger because we are made in the image of God. Anger can lead to sin in the following circumstances :

- Anger is sinful when it leads to a quick outburst of emotions. A mature christian is not to be quick-tempered or allow themselves to become suddenly so upset that they lose control of their emotions. Such people may become violent towards others or allow explosive angry outbursts to become part of their behaviour (*Proverbs 16: 32*).

- Anger is sinful when it is prolonged or continues well after the event that caused the behaviour. Paul teaches in the next verse after '*be angry and yet do not sin*', '*Do not let the sun go down on your anger, and do not give the devil an opportunity*' (*Ephesians 4:26, 27*). I do not believe this is to be taken literally – allowing you to get angry just after the sun has set so you have a whole 24 hours to stew and be angry.

- Sinful anger is also smoldering anger that may dominate a person's thinking or motivate them to seek revenge. This anger may cause someone to strike out at the person they believe has made them angry, or others who had nothing to do with the situation. Such people often carry a grudge, looking for an opportunity to get even or can induce a desire to '*pay back evil for evil*' (*Romans 12:17*). Remember the story of Cain (*Genesis 4:1 – 16*).

- Anger is sinful when a person uses angry outbursts to try to control others. Other people soon learn to be cautious when they are near that person to try to avoid their angry outbursts. Most people would rather let them have their own way instead of confronting their anger issues.

- Christians are to '*rid yourselves of these things*' (***Colossians 3:8***). Notice according to this verse, **you** are to rid yourselves of these things, not expect or pray for God to do this for you. It is your responsibility to overcome your own sinful anger.

> Anyone who seeks to grow in christian maturity and become a spiritual leader in a local church must overcome any traces of having an anger problem.

Some of the reasons why people can have a problem with anger are:

- It can be learned through a negative example (***Proverbs 22:24, 25***). The child exposed to a parent who is often violent or quick-tempered may grow up believing such behaviour is normal and behave in the same way in threatening circumstances.

- The child constantly yelled at learns to yell back, if not at parents, then at others, and the cycle of such negative behaviour may continue from generation to generation. This cycle can only be broken by the power of prayer and God's Word.

- The child who throws temper tantrums to control people and realises this gives him or her the results they want, can easily become a person who eventually throws adult temper tantrums. Such a person doesn't kick and roll around on the supermarket floor yelling or screaming, but still has temper tantrums. These are now expressed in other outward behaviours, such as yelling at others, punching the wall, slamming the door, throwing or breaking something or driving off in a huff squealing the car tyres.

- Anger can result from an insecure person who often becomes easily threatened. When challenged by friends, family, people at work or church, some insecure people can lash out in anger. Other insecure people try to become a worldly success in some career or area of life or become workaholics, or excel at church work or 'pastoring', and then desperately react with anger when someone appears to be better at it than they are.

James teaches us that righteous or Godly anger is the opposite of sinful anger (*James 1:19, 20*). Sinful or earthly anger will never achieve God's outcomes. Paul teaches us not to take revenge on others, no matter who they are or what wrongs they may have done to us, because God is the one who will avenge us (*Romans 12:17 – 21*). We do not see enough people walking around with singed hairdos today because too often we take matters into our own hands instead of having the right attitude towards those who have wronged us.

Personal application

The following personal application is designed to help you overcome sinful anger. Ask yourself the following questions as honestly as possible.

> Do I tend to get angry quickly, or have a short fuse towards people who I believe have wronged me ?

> Do I allow these angry feelings to continue towards that person (or people) long after the incident ?

> Do I want to get even with someone who made me upset or wounded me in some way ?

> Have I developed subtle ways to hurt people, other than through physical attack ?

If you answer "yes" to any of these questions, you have a sinful anger problem in your life.

Confess your sin to God and ask His forgiveness (*I John 1:9*). Be honest with God. If you have an anger problem, face it, don't pretend that it doesn't exist. Tell God how you feel, confess it as sin, and ask Him to help you overcome it.

Whatever someone may have done to you, they can never **make** you angry. Your anger is **your reaction** to the situation, and therefore it is your choice and your responsibility to overcome your anger feelings. No matter what the cause, don't blame your problem on someone else. Take responsibility for your own actions.

Make sure you are following a biblical approach to handling personal offence and forgiveness. Study carefully **Matthew 5:21 – 24** and **18:15 – 35**. What can you learn from these verses ?

Learn to overcome your problem by setting specific goals for your life in specific situations or with people who make you feel angry. Write out these goals and read them over regularly and ask God to help you achieve them.

Some suggested goals are :

➤ If you have learnt to get angry through a bad example, learn to live with Christ-like characteristics.

➤ If you are insecure and easily threatened, stop being defensive when someone challenges you. Rather, learn to listen to other people's ideas. You may find someone else has a different perspective to the problem that you could learn from.

➤ Learn to overcome your unconscious motivations that control you and cause you to strike out at others. Review the discussion above, especially regarding the lives of Cain, Moses, and Peter. What can you learn from the lives of these three men of God ?

➤ If you become angry and upset and are unable to shake the problem, learn to express your feelings in an objective and straight-ward manner. Don't brood! Communicate.

➤ Learn to back off in aggravating situations and try to look at it objectively. Why did it happen ? Ask yourself what you can do to help become a part of the solution rather than part of the problem.

➤ Memorise *James 1:19, 20* 'My dear brothers and sisters, take note of this: everyone should be quick to listen, slow to speak and slow to become angry, because human anger does not produce the righteousness that God desires.'

➤ Meditate on *Romans 12:17 – 21* every morning before you begin your day's activities, and then ask God to help you to live what this verse teaches you every day.

If you have a serious and persistent problem with anger and loss of emotional and/or physical control, and if you have not been able to overcome the problem, then you may need help from a relevant christian professional. You may need someone to help you analyse the problem and support you in overcoming it.

<u>Warning</u>: Don't expect someone else to solve your problem for you. **You** must take the initiative and become a mature person in Jesus Christ - no matter how difficult it is.

Life Quality Number 9(b) - but gentle

'*not given to drunkenness, not violent **but gentle***' (*I Timothy 3:3*).

The Greek phrase '*alla epieke*' translated as '*but gentle*' has a literal English meaning of '*gentle, mild, forbearing, fair, reasonable, moderate, mild*'[16]. Paul is teaching us a gentle christian is not quick tempered, not violent physically or verbally, but instead is respectable, reasonable, forbearing, and self-controlled.

Who should we be gentle with ?

1)   We must be gentle with those outside of God's kingdom.

Paul teaches christians to demonstrate an attitude of gentleness, not only toward other believers, but toward unbelievers. Writing to Titus, Paul teaches we are to show gentleness to everyone (*Titus 3:2*). In the next verses, he reminds us that God saved us because of His love and mercy for all of humanity, not because of any righteous works we have done (*Titus 3:4 - 6*). In other words, we must have the same love and mercy toward non-christians that God has towards us. Be as patient with their shortcomings as the Lord is with yours.

Writing to Timothy, Paul said that christians are to correct those who oppose the gospel with gentleness, if perhaps God may grant them repentance leading to the knowledge of the truth (*II Timothy 2:24, 25*).

16 - Greek word and meaning from Strong's Concordance

Paul illustrates this characteristic in his own life. *'But we were gentle among you, just as a nursing mother cherishes her own children.'* (***I Thessalonians 2:7***, NKJV). A picture of a mother nursing her baby is one of the most powerful examples of gentleness that I can think of. Paul is not ashamed to be identified with this illustration. There is no contradiction between being a man's man, a strong man and being a gentle man as far as God and Paul are concerned.

A gentle life quality will help us communicate more effectively to those outside of Christ. *'Take My yoke upon you, and learn from Me, for I am gentle and humble in heart; and you will find rest for your souls'* (***Matthew 11:29***). Our motivation with our attitude of gentleness with others, should be to help them see and then to respond to God's love for them just as we responded to God's love for us.

Very few people ever respond to God by anyone 'Bible bashing' or pointing out that they are a sinner going to hell. Most people already know their life is a mess and they are searching for the answers. You and I should be able to lovingly point them to the God that has the answers, rather than bringing them into more condemnation.

2)   We must be gentle with christians who have sinned.

'Therefore, as God's chosen people, holy and dearly loved, clothe yourselves with compassion, kindness, humility, gentleness and patience. Bear with each other and forgive one another if any of you has a grievance against someone. Forgive as the Lord forgave you.' (***Colossians 3:12, 13***). Notice the phrase 'as the Lord forgave you' !

'Brothers and sisters, if someone is caught in a sin, you who live by the Spirit should restore that person gently. But watch yourselves, or you also may be tempted. Carry eachother's burdens, and in this way you will fulfill the law of Christ.' (***Galatians 6:1, 2***)

84

All believers need to read again Jesus' story of the unjust slave who, though forgiven by his master, failed to forgive his fellow slave (*Matthew 18:21 - 35*). The unjust slave was tormented because of his unforgiveness, just as some christian people are tormented today because of their unforgiveness.

> Paul reminds us that our gentleness, patience, and kindness are to be based on the Lord's attitude towards us. How can we, who have experienced the marvellous grace and forgiveness of God, fail to forgive those who sin against us?

As you read other words of Paul, you will note that his attitude was always one of deep concern. He disciplined in love! *"By the humility and gentleness of Christ, I appeal to you"* (*II Corinthians 10:1*). This is to be the attitude of mature christians toward a brother or sister who has failed in their christian life. There should never be any room for pride, superiority, resentment, or judgement (*James 5:19, 20*).

3)   We must be gentle with every christian person we know, especially as a leader. Christians are to relate to all other christians with humility and gentleness, with patience, bearing with one another in love (*Ephesians 4:2, 3*).

Gentleness does not equal weakness. Only a strong person can truly be a gentle person in all circumstances. Gentleness is a quality that God wants to produce in your life through the Holy Spirit and His Word. *'But the fruit of the Spirit is love, joy, peace, forbearance, kindness, goodness, faithfulness, gentleness and self-control. Against such things there is no law.'* (*Galatians 5:22, 23*).

To experience the fruit of the Spirit, we must walk by the Spirit (*Galatians 5:25*). You must consciously and deliberately put off or abandon the deeds of the flesh and walk in the way God has outlined in His Word. Gentleness and all the other qualities outlined in *Galatians chapter 5* do not automatically drop out of heaven and envelop or control our emotions when we become a christian. The fruit of the Spirit must be developed through the process of becoming more and more like Jesus Christ in our daily lives.

God is ready to give wisdom to His children to enable us to walk by the Spirit. '*If any of you lacks wisdom, you should ask God, who gives generously to all without finding fault, and it will be given to you. But when you ask, you must believe and not doubt, because the one who doubts is like a wave of the sea, blown and tossed by the wind. That person should not expect to receive anything from the Lord. Such a person is double-minded and unstable in all they do.*' (*James 1:5 - 8*).

'*But you, man of God, flee from all this, and pursue righteousness, godliness, faith, love, endurance and gentleness*' (*I Timothy 6:11*). Gentleness must be a goal for every christian just as any other spiritual quality. Fortunately for some people, being gentle is an easy or natural character trait. Unfortunately for many of us, being gentle is a difficult character trait to exhibit in our daily lives.

Personal application

The following personal application is designed to help you develop the quality of gentleness in all your relationships.

Think about those relationships in life where you have the most difficulty demonstrating gentleness. Set up goals as you ask God to give you wisdom to become the person you should be in these relationships. The following suggestions may help you identify and isolate your problem areas :

➢ If you are married, ask your wife (or husband, ladies) and children to help make you aware of times when you are not gentle. Sometimes we do not really know how we sound to others.

➢ Ask a close friend to frankly evaluate your relationships with other people, to give you feedback on any area that violates a spirit of gentleness.

➢ If you are a teacher, a boss, or anyone who works with people, ask them to fill out an evaluation form. Include a question regarding how they see your attitudes and behaviour. Ask them to evaluate the spirit in which you do things, such as the way you give orders, make assignments or answer questions.

➢ Develop a regular Bible study program. There is no substitute for the scriptures to reveal to us those areas which do not truly show the reality of Jesus Christ to others we may encounter in our daily lives.

Life Quality Number 10 -
Not quarrelsome

'*not given to drunkenness, not violent but gentle, **not quarrelsome***'
(*I Timothy 3:3*)

'Since an overseer manages God's household, he must be blameless - ***not overbearing***' (*Titus 1:7*)

There are many similarities in the meaning of the English words '*quarrelsome*' and '*overbearing*'. Some people use these interchangeably or think that these two English words essentially have the same meaning.

In *I Timothy 3:3* and *Titus 1:7*, Paul deliberately uses two different Greek words which are translated as the English words '*quarrelsome*' and '*overbearing*'. The Greek word '*amachos*' translated as '*not quarrelsome*' in *I Timothy 3:3*, has a literal English meaning of '*peaceable, abstaining from fighting, not contentious*'. In *Titus 1:7*, the Greek word '*authadés*' translated as '*overbearing*' has a literal English meaning of '*self-satisfied, self-pleasing, arrogant, stubborn*'[17].

In this book '*not quarrelsome*' and '*not overbearing*' are discussed as two separate life qualities, due to the differences between these two words in the Greek text.

This life quality '*not quarrelsome*' has some overlap with two other life qualities discussed in this book, Number 9b '*but gentle*' (being kind to everyone) and Number 7 '*being able to teach*'. You should refer to these life qualities in this book for further information regarding these two life qualities.

---

17 - Greek words and meanings from Strong's Concordance

'Don't have anything to do with foolish and stupid arguments, because you know they produce quarrels. And the Lord's servant must not be quarrelsome but must be kind to everyone, able to teach, not resentful.' (**II Timothy 2:23, 24**). Paul uses another Greek word '*maché*' translated as '*quarrelsome*' in verse 23, which has a literal English meaning of '*fight, strife, a battle, conflict, contention, dispute, quarrel*'[18]. The context of these verses refers to people who oppose true Biblical teaching.

Paul was teaching Timothy, and us in the 21st century, that mature christians must avoid starting or continuing arguments or quarrels to show everyone how smart they think they are or how much Bible knowledge they may have, or think they have. They don't look down upon or make others feel inferior to their 'superior' Bible knowledge. Scriptures should never be used by mature christians to prove that 'I am right, and you are wrong' in a 'holier than you' attitude. Instead, mature christians are to be gentle, sensitive, and respectful to other people, even those who are confused or even hostile, obstinate, or bitter to Biblical teaching.

I knew a christian man in a church I attended who was an intelligent, successful businessman. He would spend many of his lunch breaks from work in the local park praying to God and put many of us so called spiritual people to shame!

If he was 'calling the shots' and 'making all the decisions', he was happy, easy to live with, and cooperative. When he was just one among equals, it was a different story. He always seemed to take an opposite viewpoint to everyone else during church members meetings. If it was his idea, fine! But if the idea came from someone else, he could never seem to get excited about it. He would do all he could to find reasons why it wouldn't work. Whenever a vote on an issue was taken - it was usually his against everyone else's.

---

18 - Greek word and meaning from Strong's Concordance

That was confusing for me to understand until I started studying the Biblical teaching about a quarrelsome person. I then understood that even though this man spent more time in prayer than most of us ever did, he was still quarrelsome. He could not stand competition and was unwilling to bend or compromise on any issue, because it was either his way or no way. Compromising for the sake of peace within the members meetings was not in his character. He was causing divisions and destroying any unity in that church.

The words of Jesus Christ in *Matthew 23:11*, '*The greatest among you will be your servant*' , teach us that true biblical leadership in the church is the opposite of the way the world sees leadership. There is to be no authoritarian figure running the whole show. Leaders, yes - but as part of a team. Someone who may put in more time and effort, and even be financially remunerated, but as one among equals. This the opposite of the quarrelsome nature of my christian friend discussed above.

When it comes to the functioning body of Christ, no concept is more important in the scriptures than unity. No concern is more upon the heart of Jesus Christ Himself! Knowing that the time was quickly coming for Him to complete the work He had come to do on earth, He prayed in earnest to the Father for His disciples - and for us.

'My prayer is not for them alone. I pray also for those who will believe in me through their message, that all of them may be one, Father, just as you are in me and I am in you. May they also be in us so that the world may believe that you have sent me. I have given them the glory that you gave me, that they may be one as we are one - I in them and you in me - so that they may be brought to complete unity. Then the world will know that you sent me and have loved them even as you have loved me.' (**John 17:20 - 23**).

I believe quarrelsome people are condemned in scripture because they often cause divisions within the body of Christ which can destroy christian unity and witness in the local area.

Christian church unity demonstrates to the world the deity of Jesus Christ and the unity He has with God the Father and the Holy Spirit. God is particularly pleased with those individuals who strive to create unity. *'Blessed are the peace-makers,'* said Jesus, *'for they shall be called children of God'* (**Matthew 5:9**).

'As a prisoner for the Lord, then, I urge you to live a life worthy of the calling you have received. Be completely humble and gentle; be patient, bearing with one another in love. Make every effort to keep the unity of the Spirit through the bond of peace.' (**Ephesians 4:1 - 3**).

Quarrelsome people struggle against and compete with others, love debating (if they get their own way all the time) and are often insecure in their personality or self-image. Insecure people may respond to circumstances they perceive as threatening in one of three different ways :

1)   Some people are reclusive and withdrawn. They seldom open their mouths and retreat from any kind of competition. They have a problem with authority – they will never exercise what may be their God-given calling and ability.

2)   Some people become domineering and authoritarian to cover up their insecurity by controlling everyone else, often putting other people down, to build themselves up. They can't accept defeat, so they become winners and often overachieve and then work frantically to stay on top. When their position is threatened in any way, they react by being argumentative, quarrelsome, gossipers and backbiters, and may use critical remarks or physical violence to defend themselves against their fear of failure.

If they are in christian leadership, these people tend to rationalise their behaviour and may use God's Word as a weapon to reach their self-centred goals. They interpret scripture for their own means and take advantage of their ' spiritual ' position by lording it over others. If anyone resists their authoritarian tactics, they quickly try to control their opponents by labelling them as rebellious or with words such as "Obey your leaders and submit to them" (which is conveniently misinterpreted from *Hebrews 13:7*).

3)   Some people become bitter, either against God or others, or both, and direct their bitterness against those who they feel are against them. A person with a bitter spirit often has a 'chip on the shoulder' attitude that may also affect other people and can destroy a church from within. '*Make every effort to live in peace with everyone and to be holy; without holiness no one will see the Lord. See to it that no one falls short of the grace of God and that no bitter root grows up to cause trouble and defile many.*' (*Hebrews 12:14, 15*)

In contrast to christian leaders who lord it over others or rule for their own person gain, Peter appeals to the leaders of God's people to be shepherds who are willing and eager to serve for God's glory.

'To the elders among you, I appeal as a fellow elder and a witness of Christ's sufferings who also will share in the glory to be revealed: Be shepherds of God's flock that is under your care, watching over them— not because you must, but because you are willing, as God wants you to be; not pursuing dishonest gain, but eager to serve; not lording it over those entrusted to you, but being examples to the flock. And when the Chief Shepherd appears, you will receive the crown of glory that will never fade away.' (*I Peter 5:1 – 4*)

Are you a christian leader who will receive the crown of glory from the Chief Shepherd ?

Personal application

The following personal application is designed to help you recognise and overcome any quarrelsome attitudes in your personality. Ask yourself the following questions and read again the above discussion on this life quality.

➤ Am I quarrelsome because of my insecurity ?

➤ Am I quarrelsome because I am jealous of someone else's success ?

➤ Am I quarrelsome because I am bitter or blame God or someone else for my lack of success ?

If you sense you have a quarrelsome attitude towards anyone, you need to begin a process of change.

➤ Start with confession. First to God and then to those you have hurt, if appropriate. If you have hurt anyone in the local body of Christ in which you fellowship, confess your sin to the other person or people involved, if appropriate, and ask for their forgiveness and prayers so that you might change your attitudes and behaviour.

➤ Public confession should be made only if it has affected the whole body, and please seek advice from the spiritual leaders in your church as to whether or not public confession or private confession to those you have hurt is necessary.

➤ Write out specific goals which relate to your specific problem with specific people. Read these goals every day and use them as personal prayer requests.

Life Quality Number 11 - Not a lover of money

'*not given to drunkenness, not violent but gentle, not quarrelsome,*
not a lover of money.' (*I Timothy 3:2, 3*)

Titus 1:7 '*not to pursue dishonest gain*'.

'*Not a lover of money*' refers to valuing money or material possessions above God and eternal treasures, rather than the motives or methods of obtaining these things (which is '*pursuing dishonest gain*' and discussed as a separate life quality, number 15, in this book).

In the parable of the widow's mite, (*Mark 12:43*), Jesus teaches us it is not what we give that matters in terms of dollars - but our attitude to giving that counts. The widow gave all she had, because she had an attitude that God would provide for her every need.

'*Those who want to get rich fall into temptation and a trap and into many foolish and harmful desires that plunge people into ruin and destruction. For the love of money is a root of all kinds of evil. Some people, eager for money, have wandered from the faith and pierced themselves with many griefs.*' (*I Timothy 6:9, 10*).

There are many stories of people who have a lot of money, who pass away and then family members are in court fighting over who would get what out of their estate. Families are torn apart by a rich relative's estate (or when someone happens to strike it rich from Lotto, Pokies, Casket, Horses, or other gambling pursuits) because of jealousy. The love of money in these cases is the true root of the evil that separates many family members.

Money in itself is not evil, nor is having a healthy bank account. The Bible does not say a christian should be 'free from money' but rather, 'not a **lover** of money.' It is a matter of priorities.

> You can still be a lover of money even if you do not have much money in the bank.

Obviously, all of us need money to exist in our culture and country. When we make money for selfish purposes or self-glorification, we are building on a shaky foundation. Remember Jesus parable of the rich fool (*Luke 12:13 - 21*) ? Gaining the whole world or all the money in the bank but losing your soul is just not worth it.

The love of money or wanting more and more material possessions for yourself or your family, is often the underlying driver for a person to pursue or chase lucrative opportunities, even if they are questionable in their means or involve a so-called 'grey area'.

This Life Quality is about the lifestyle of a person who is more earthly minded than heavenly minded and not about how many dollars you have in the bank. How many times have you thought that if I just had a few extra thousand dollars my life's problems would be overcome (but maybe never said out loud) ? This sort of attitude, either said out loud or secretly thought, defines a person who is a lover of money.

A person who loves money lays up treasures upon earth rather than treasures in heaven (*Matthew 6:19 - 21*).

'*Keep your lives free from the love of money and be content with what you have, because God has said, "Never will I leave you; never will I forsake you.*" (*Hebrews 13:5*).

'*Above all else, guard your heart, for everything you do flows from it.*' (**Proverbs 4:23**). Your heart or the motivation of your life is where your treasures are, or what you put your energies into to try to achieve. The lover of money considers this present life, its worldly possessions, activities, and benefits are more important than eternal life. There is constant seeking after more and more money and material possessions which can become an end in themselves rather than a means to Godly ends.

'*Two things I ask of you, LORD; do not refuse me before I die: Keep falsehood and lies far from me; give me neither poverty nor riches, but give me only my daily bread. Otherwise, I may have too much and disown you and say, 'Who is the LORD ?' Or I may become poor and steal, and so dishonour the name of my God.*' (**Proverbs 30:7 - 9**).

The problem of forgetting God when earthly possessions multiply is not new. The children of Israel faced this temptation when they entered the Promised Land. Moses warned them ahead of time that this temptation would come. '*When the Lord your God brings you into the land he swore to your fathers, to Abraham, Isaac and Jacob, to give you—a land with large, flourishing cities you did not build, houses filled with all kinds of good things you did not provide, wells you did not dig, and vineyards and olive groves you did not plant—then when you eat and are satisfied, be careful that you do not forget the Lord, who brought you out of Egypt, out of the land of slavery.*' (**Deuteronomy 6:10 - 12**). Despite of the warnings by Moses, that is exactly what happened after Joshua died (**Judges 2:10 – 13**).

We as christians in the 21st Century need to learn a basic lesson from Israel. <u>God's material blessings upon us can also become a curse.</u>

Someone may start out in life with relatively little. As he or she starts to accumulate a certain amount of wealth, he or she soon learns that 'money talks', it attracts 'friends' and gives status, and security. As soon as the money is gone, the friends and associated status disappear. Jesus taught this in the parable about the prodigal son (*Luke 15:11 - 32*).

We have been brought up and brain washed by advertising (especially on TV) that makes us **feel** we need certain things to be happy, comfortable, successful, or desirable. This is naturally true of children, though it is also true of adults. We cannot ignore these feelings, as they are real. It takes wisdom to strike a proper balance in our materialistic culture between worldly possessions and the **love** of worldly possessions.

To give children too much creates problems, but to withhold what is 'normal' also creates problems. When we try to teach a child to become non-materialistic by withholding material things that are continually at the disposal of most of their peers, it may only serve to create an unsatisfied thirst for material things. Every parent needs to have a balance in this area of their child's life.

Some people take pride in their poverty. They justify their lack of work or laziness to prove they are not loving money. Other people think and teach that the poorer you are and the more you must rely on other people to provide for your daily necessities, the more spiritual you are. Obviously, this is not what the Lord had in mind!

'*For even when we were with you, we gave you this rule: "The one who is unwilling to work shall not eat." We hear that some among you are idle and disruptive. They are not busy; they are busybodies. Such people we command and urge in the Lord Jesus Christ to settle down and earn the food they eat.*' (**II Thessalonians 3:10 - 12**).

Some of the religious leaders of Ezekiel's time were more interested in fleecing the flock of God than taking care of it (*Ezekiel 34:1 – 10*).

Unfortunately, the twenty-first century church world is also filled with what I call 'religious hustlers' who take advantage of other christians financially. Religious hustlers often resort to guilt tactics, 'don't you feel sorry for me' innuendos to get money. These people may make statements such as "if you don't give to this 'urgent need from the Lord' then you are not really committed to following Him" or "this important 'project from the Lord' or what the 'Lord has called me to do' will fail if you don't give enough". As if His work is dependent on us anyway !!!!!

(If asked or confronted with such or similar statements from christian people what do you do or say ? I suggest that you simply say – "It sure is an urgent need and I'll join with you in prayer to see that need met, but I can't commit myself (or my church) financially at this time until I seek the Lord's will about the matter").

Other tactics may include trying to shame or intimidate people to give more by taking up a second or third or fourth offering until the amount is what 'the Lord had told me before I came' or by saying things like 'give till it hurts' (it is usually made to hurt the giver and not the receiver) or even scolding people if they did not give enough.

Paul was cautious not be associated with such religious hustlers. He was genuinely concerned that people know the gospel was free, and often did his best to be a good example.

'*What then is my reward ? Just this: that in preaching the gospel I may offer it free of charge, and so not make full use of my rights as a preacher of the gospel.*' (*I Corinthians 9:18 ; Acts 18:1 - 3* and *20: 33 - 35*).

To become a lover of money is a temptation for ministers who may become focused on the offering total instead of God's work. Eventually this may lead to the focus of church meetings being on the money, with sermons and promotions designed to 'encourage' those attending to dig deep for the 'work of the Lord'.

It must be made clear, however, that it is God's will for spiritual leaders to be cared for financially by those who are taught.

'The elders who direct the affairs of the church well are worthy of double honour, especially those whose work is preaching and teaching.' (*I Timothy 5:17*). Paul is obviously referring here to material remuneration. To the Corinthians he also made it clear that those who proclaim the gospel should '*receive their living from the gospel*' (*I Corinthians 9:14*).

However, a word also needs to be said to put this into perspective. Some christians take advantage of christian leaders who make their living from full-time ministry. They somehow feel that a pastor or missionary shouldn't be paid as much as the average person. (They would not dream of having a job with less than such and such a pay packet but become resentful and critical when they find out that the minister receives a similar pay packet).

Some even go so far as to think a christian leader should serve without remuneration to be kept 'humble' and 'dependant on God by faith'. Numerous christian leaders have experienced the time when the remuneration they received for christian ministry did not cover their travel expenses. This, of course, is just as wrong as a spiritual leader who is a lover of money.

For many christian ministers, the temptation to make more money from business or job promotions and extra overtime is very real. To balance the material needs of providing for family living expenses and spending quality time with church work is extremely hard where the church support is lacking or only a token measure. This is especially true of smaller churches or those who are struggling financially. Often the first thing to get cut is the minister's pay! <u>This is also inconsistent with Paul's teaching.</u>

When my wife and I were pastoring a small church, we felt lead by God to close our church for a Sunday morning service and take all of our people that would come to another small church about 1 hour drive away to conduct the Sunday morning service. We would provide the music, songs and preaching so that this other small church could be blessed, and we encouraged our people to bring their offering to bless this other church financially as well.

When we approached the minister of the other small church, his first reaction was 'what are we going to do with the offering ?' He had the attitude that the most important reason the people came on Sunday was so that they could give money to meet the church (and his) expenses. <u>This attitude is also inconsistent with Paul's teaching.</u>

Personal application

The following personal application is designed to help you evaluate your motives regarding money and material things.

Make a list of those things that are most important to you in your life right now. Write down those things that first appear in your mind. Be as honest as you can, and do not over spiritualise these either. You also need to be as specific and detailed as possible. These are your priorities in life right now. Think about what you have written and consider each one in the light of biblical values.

➢ What motivates you the most ?

➢ What are you doing with your money ?

➢ Do you really believe that God can supply all your needs (including material) ? (*Read Philippians 4:10 - 19*)

➢ Can you justify your expenditures in the light of eternal values ?

➢ How much are you giving away for worthy causes compared to what you spend on life's luxuries ?

Carefully read the following passages of scripture to help you rearrange your priorities :

- *Proverbs 15:27*
- *Proverbs 23:4, 5*
- *Proverbs 30:7 - 9*
- *Ecclesiastes 5:10 - 12*

- *Matthew 19:16 – 26*
- *Luke 16:10 – 16*
- *I Timothy 6:6 – 10*

In the light of this study and personal evaluation, set up specific goals for your life relative to 'money matters'. No one can tell you what to do specifically except God. The following Biblical principles may help guide you in this area :

> The 'love of money' is sin; that is, to value money or material possessions more than spiritual things or to accumulate money for purely personal gain or advantage.

> To obtain money in deceitful or dishonest ways is a violation of God's laws.

> Every christian is to give regularly and promptly according to the way God has prospered him or her.

> Christians are to use their material possessions to care for other christians who are in need.

> Do you ever get resentful when you must pay for another christian's expenses ?

> Christians are not to be lazy and irresponsible, 'bludging' off other people. This is sin.

Life Quality Number 12 -
Manage his own family well

'*He must **manage his own family well** and see that his children obey him, and he must do so in a manner worthy of full respect. (If anyone does not know how to manage his own family, how can he take care of God's church ?)*' (*I Timothy 3:4, 5.*)

Titus 1:6 '*a man whose children believe and are not open to the charge of being wild and disobedient.*'

This life quality refers to the home life of a mature Christian leader, rather than successful christian ministry to others.

Many pastors, missionaries, and lay leaders are well known for their achievements in christian work. They have built large churches, led many to Jesus Christ, and are very active in the church. On the surface they appear to be very successful christian leaders.

However, in some instances, their own sons and daughters grow up rejecting Jesus Christ and resenting christian work because it has taken their father and/or mother away from them. In their eyes, their parents were always too busy or away preaching to be involved in their important activities such as school awards ceremonies or sports days.

To understand more specifically what Paul means by this life quality, it is helpful to first understand what I believe he **does not mean**.

❑ It is not necessary to have children to be a spiritual leader in the church, nor to be a mature Godly person.

- Paul is teaching that if a person is married, and if he has children, he is to have a well-ordered household. An additional implication is that if a man does become a spiritual leader before he has a family, and then fails to measure up to Paul's criteria, he then would cease to be qualified to continue as a spiritual leader in the church.

- Paul is not referring to a perfect family. As there is no 'perfect church', so there is no 'perfect family'. There is no perfect husband or father, no perfect wife or mother, and no perfect children.

- All christians will have problems in their family life. Satan will see to that while we are in this world. We should strive towards having a family that is as free as possible from problems. Just as every christian is in the process of becoming more and more like Jesus Christ, so should every family be in the process of growing spiritually.

- No one is automatically disqualified from being a church leader because they have some children who do not follow the Lord or attend church. The Greek word, 'pista' translated as 'believe' in **Titus 1:6** has a literal English meaning of 'trustworthy, trustful, believing, or believer, faithful(-ly), sure, true'[19]. There are many instances of pastor's kids who are decent, in order, well controlled and respectful but who do NOT follow God. Each of us, including our own kids, has the choice to follow Christ or reject Him. We must also remember the wayward or backslidden son or daughter often comes back to God later in life.

---

19 - Greek word and meaning from Strong's Concordance

❑ Paul is not referring here to small children. There are several Greek words used to describe children in the New Testament. The Greek word, '*teknon*', Paul uses in *I Timothy 3* and in *Titus 1* is a general word used for 'offspring'[20]. This word, of course, could be used to refer to small children, but the total context in which Paul uses the word seems to indicate 'grown' children[21]. Paul uses the same Greek word when referring to 'mature children' who are responsible to provide for their mother's material needs in *I Timothy 5:4* [22]. In Titus, Paul specifies that a person chosen for spiritual leadership in the church must have children who are faithful, not accused of being wild or disobedient, which are both characteristics true only of older children.

❑ Paul is not referring to the normal patterns of child growth and development. Small children often go through natural phases that have sometimes been wrongly interpreted as the kind of 'rebellion' Paul is referring to in *Titus 1:6.*

I believe Paul is referring to the home life or household of a mature christian leader. Where the whole household is committed to Jesus Christ, a wife who is dedicated to her husband, and grown children who respect and love their father, you have strong evidence that their parents are spiritually and psychologically mature. They will certainly be able to 'take care of God's church'.

---

20 - Guthrie et al (1976)

21 - Guthrie et al (1976)

22 - Thayer (1979)

However, where this is not true, problems may occur if a man or woman is appointed as a church leader. The difficulties in their household or home life are likely to be reflected in the church. If he or she accepts a church leadership position, the family members are often likely to have less respect for them, resulting in even greater problems in the home. In other words, we can make life worse for an individual by ignoring this important criterion for maturity and church leadership potential.

> Paul viewed the well-ordered home as the true test of a someone's maturity and ability to lead other christians, especially a home that has passed the test of time.

To be a good husband and father, wife, or mother, to have a well-ordered household, should be a goal for every christian parent.

All christian husbands are to love their wives *'just as Christ also loved the church'* (**Ephesians 5:25**). They are to live with them *'in an understanding way'* and to grant them *'honour as a fellow heir to the grace of life.'* (**I Peter 3:7**). Peter suggests in the rest of this verse that a man who does not live this way will have hindered (unanswered) prayers. Fathers are not to provoke their children but to *'bring them up in the discipline and instruction of the Lord'* (**Ephesians 6:4**).

Paul compared his own actions to a father behaving toward his children when he encouraged, comforted, and urged others to live lives that pleased God (**I Thessalonians 2:11, 12**). This illustration, of course, shows how Paul viewed the father's responsibility to the children.

110

The 'father image' is an important concept in scripture. We tell our children God is our heavenly father, and they quickly make a comparison. God, who is Spirit and invisible to a child, automatically takes on the same characteristics as an earthly father. If a father is kind and loving, so is God, in the mind of a child. However, if dad is cold and cruel, so is God. That is why the way we live our life in front of our children is so important.

This is especially true when dealing with pastor's kids. If all that they ever hear is the problems and criticisms of certain church members at home, that is the attitude that they will grow up with. This is often the major cause of pastor's kids backsliding.

If all they ever hear are the good points of all the people in church, then that is what they will grow up believing. (If you have any criticisms of a brother or sister, please do not display them in front of your children. Discuss them after the kids have gone to bed and then deal with them if needed according to scripture verses such as *Matthew chapter 18*).

Kids soon learn if the motive for their standards of behaviour set at home are for their good or for their parent's or the church's reputation! Some spiritual leaders come down too hard on their children. They try to get their teenagers to conform to certain behavioural patterns in order so that they, the spiritual leaders, are not criticised by other christians in the church.

Now, make no mistake! Children of christian leaders should certainly be good examples. However, they should also be allowed to be 'normal' both by parents and by christians in the church. They resent a 'higher standard' simply because their dad and/or mum happens to be the pastor or a leader and resent being told to 'be good' so their dad and/or mum 'looks good'. Ultimately, this kind of motivation will backfire; even creating 'rebellion' rather than 'cooperation'.

I like the approach of one pastor who overheard his son being reprimanded by an elder in the church. The elder who was criticising his son said something like this : "I certainly expect more from you than that, young man, being the preacher's son." The pastor immediately took the elder aside and, in no uncertain terms, let him know he never wanted that type of reprimand to happen again. "If my son is out of order" he said, "come to me and I'll discipline him. If he needs immediate discipline and I am not available, don't ever use my position as a weapon against him." He was not defending his son, but he didn't want his son to feel he was under some kind of 'performance standard' just because he was the 'preacher's kid.'

When our message does not conform to our daily lives we are in serious trouble with our children, and we are in danger of driving them away from Jesus Christ; the very one we want them to serve. It is easy to fool other people regarding our spirituality, but we can't fool our wives, our husbands, or our children. They live with us twenty-four hours a day, seven days a week and know us as we really are.

Personal application

The following personal application is designed to help you become a good husband and father or wife and mother and to have a well-managed household.

For those who have a family with or without children

Ask your wife (or husband) to read this lesson on a well-managed household, and help you evaluate your ability to manage your family. The following questions may help you.

1) How can I become a better husband (or wife) ?

- ➤ What are my strengths ?
- ➤ What are my weaknesses ?

2) How can I become a better father (or mother) ?

- ➤ What are my strengths ?
- ➤ What are my weaknesses ?

To develop biblical goals for developing a Godly family, study the following passages:

• *Deuteronomy 6:4-9*   • *Ephesians. 5:25 - 33*   • *Philippians 2:1 - 18*

Set up specific goals for developing a well-managed household. Base these goals on actual weaknesses you may have learnt about yourself through the discussion above on this life quality. As you do, be sure to include your wife (or husband) in your planning. Pray together asking God to give you wisdom to overcome your weaknesses. You may also want to include your children in helping you to set up goals which draw you closer together as a family.

For those who have never married

Evaluate your relationship with your own father (or mother) using the discussion above. What lessons can you learn to improve your ability to manage family relationships now and in the future ?

For those who are divorced, or single parents, with or without children

➤ Evaluate your relationship with your children (if you have children). How can you be a better parent to your children, even if you only see them part-time ?

➤ How do you talk about your partner in front of others (and/or your children) ? Do you blame that partner or God for the situation you now have ?

➤ Can you see your situation as an opportunity for God to show his love and mercy to you and to others ?

➤ Where you can, try to show your children or speak to them about God's love, even though they and you are in a difficult situation.

Life Quality Number 13 - Not a recent convert

*'He must **not be a recent convert**, or he may become conceited and fall under the same judgment as the devil.'* (*I Timothy 3:6*)

Immediately after his dramatic conversion experience, Saul, on his way to becoming Paul the apostle, preached in the Jewish Synagogues in Damascus. The result was that he had to escape death by being lowered in a basket in the wall at night (*Acts 9:20 - 25*). Then he left Jerusalem (*Acts 9:28 - 30*) because of the plans of some devout Jews to kill him. After three years he spent 15 days with Peter, and then it was 14 years later before he finally met with the leaders in Jerusalem to discuss the beginning of his ministry to the Gentiles. (*Galatians 1:18 - 24 and 2:1 – 10*). During his time away from the spotlight, Paul learnt all the wonderful teaching from God that he shares with us in his letters in the New Testament, such as ***Romans, I*** and ***II Corinthians, Galatians,*** and ***Ephesians***.

One of the of the trends among christian leaders in recent years that I find disturbing is to encourage new or recent converts to experience instant popularity as a christian. This is particularly true regarding individuals who have prominent worldly positions, such as converted rock star musicians, athletes, movie stars, drug dealers or satanists and any others who fall into the 'chief sinners' category. Though the majority of christian leaders may mean well, unfortunately some seem to use a new convert as either a publicity stunt to attract large crowds for meetings (motive is publicity) or to demonstrate to prospective donors what God is doing through their ministry or organisation (motive is for more sponsorship dollars).

The previous year's rising star is not mentioned much anymore and may become disillusioned, backslide, or drop out of anything to do with christianity. Many of these new converts have survived this experience; but others have been shipwrecked, as they have simply become pawns in the battle for sponsorship dollars or christian popularity or have fallen away when they became proud of their own christain testimony or achievements.

A new convert doesn't have the time or experiences to develop the life qualities of a mature Godly person. He or she may have lots of experience in some profession, or he or she may be an incredibly talented musician, actor, or sportsman. If promoted and appointed in a leadership position too early, he or she may not have developed the Godly characteristics in their life that are necessary for such positions in the local church.

Paul's concern is that new converts do not have enough experience to serve as an elder or leader in the church because they can easily become proud or develop an unbalanced view of their own importance.

The Greek word, 'typhōtheis' translated into the English phrase 'become conceited' in *I Timothy 3:6*, has a literal English meaning of '*to become blinded by pride, be inflated with self-conceit*'[23]. Most Bible commentaries, such as Barnes notes and Matthew Henry's commentary, suggest Paul's words warn of the danger of a new christian, or newly planted or newly converted one, becoming proud, and thus falling into the same condemnation from God as the devil. Matthew Henry's commentary states '*pride turned angles into devils*'.

---

23 - *Word and meaning from Strong's Concordance*

To give any new or recent convert too much prominence as a christian until he or she has developed some characteristics of maturity, I believe, is to help satan create pride that eventually leads to their personal downfall and failure. This does not mean, of course, that a recent convert cannot participate as a member of the body of Christ, sharing their talents, testimony, and life, and be a blessing to the church as well as lead others to find Christ as their saviour. It does mean that overexposure focusing on someone's personality or talents, may cause such a person to become proud, to feel he is a 'special gift' from God to the christian community. This is the very reason a new convert may come under the same judgement as the devil.

Satan is the ultimate source of pride. He was originally in God's very presence but became arrogant and boastful when he challenged God. As a result, he fell from his lofty position (*Isaiah 14:12 - 17*). Satan is just waiting, implies Paul, to take advantage of new converts, and the apostle warns against helping him achieve his ends.

Paul gives a similar warning in *I Timothy 6:3, 4* '*If anyone teaches otherwise and does not consent to wholesome words, even the words of our Lord Jesus Christ, and to the doctrine which accords with godliness, he is proud, knowing nothing, ...*'. (NKJV)

Both James and Peter refer to *Proverbs 3:34* when they wrote '*God opposes the proud but shows favour to the humble*' (*James 4:6* and *I Peter 5:5 - 7*).

Pride has ruined far too many christian people. It was a major sin in Israel's history, for they were warned that when they entered the promised land and received for nothing all of the natural blessings God gave them, they may become proud and take credit for it themselves (*Deuteronomy 8:14*). This is exactly what they did, which resulted in their downfall time after time after time as recorded in the book of Judges.

King Uzziah was severely judged by God in his later life because *'his pride led to his downfall'* (**II Chronicles 26:16**). Hezekiah, too, was judged *'because his heart was proud'* (**II Chronicles 32:24 - 26**). Note that when he *'repented of the pride of his heart'*, he was again blessed by God. These verses also show us that God's wrath can be on a nation because of the pride of their leader.

It takes time to develop all the characteristics of a mature man or woman of God. I believe that is why Paul explains his experiences in **Romans chapter 7:14** to **8:1**. In **II Corinthians 12:7-10**, Paul teaches us he had a problem (thorn in the flesh) that God continued to allow so that he did not become too proud of his own achievements. Maybe some of us need a similar thorn in the flesh for the same reason ?

Any christian, no matter how mature, can become a victim of satan's darts of pride in his achievements or church status. How easy it is to become proud of human accomplishments, to take credit for what belongs to God! Since the beginning of christianity, people have tried to take credit for their own salvation, which leads to pride and self-righteousness. *'Pride goes before destruction, and a haughty spirit before a fall'* (**Proverbs 16:18**).

Where pride comes into a person's life, God goes out. Conversely, where God comes into a person's life, pride goes out.

Personal application

The following personal application is designed to help you avoid becoming proud.

After reading over the material above, honestly answer the following questions :

➤ Am I a proud person – do I think out loud or inside of me that the church cannot function without me or that God's work could not succeed unless I am part of it ?

➤ Can I see others receiving the glory for something I did, said, or initiated and NOT be adversely affected ?

➤ What do I say to God when someone I have trained has learnt the job so well that they can now do it better than I can, or are now in a 'better church' position than I am ?

Read and study the following scriptures to see if you can learn more about the danger of pride in your christian life.

II Chronicles 25:19
Proverbs 18:12
II Chronicles 32:25
Proverbs 21:4
Psalm 101:5
Romans 12:16
Psalm 138:6
James 4:6, 7
Proverbs 16:5

Life Quality Number 14 -
A good reputation with outsiders

'*He must also have a **good reputation with outsiders**, so that he will not fall into disgrace and into the devil's trap.*' (*I Timothy 3:7*)

Carefully consider the following scripture verses :

'*A good name is more desirable than great riches,* ' (***Proverbs 22:1***).

'*Slaves, obey your earthly masters with respect and fear, and with sincerity of heart, just as you would obey Christ. Obey them not only to win their favour when their eye is on you, but as slaves of Christ, doing the will of God from your heart. Serve wholeheartedly, as if you were serving the Lord, not people, because you know that the Lord will reward each one for whatever good they do, whether they are slave or free. And masters, treat your slaves in the same way. Do not threaten them, since you know that he who is both their Master and yours is in heaven, and there is no favouritism with him.*' (***Ephesians 6:5 – 9***).

'*Do everything without grumbling or arguing, so that you may become blameless and pure, 'children of God without fault in a warped and crooked generation'. Then you will shine among them like stars in the sky*' (***Philippians 2:14, 15***)

'*Be wise in the way you act toward outsiders; make the most of every opportunity. Let your conversation be always full of grace, seasoned with salt, so that you may know how to answer everyone.*' (***Colossians 4:5, 6***) *'make it your ambition to lead a quiet life: You should mind your own business and work with your hands, just as we told you, so that your daily life may win the respect of outsiders and so that you will not be dependent on anybody.'* (*I Thessalonians 4:11, 12*)

'Live such good lives among the pagans that, though they accuse you of doing wrong, they may see your good deeds and glorify God on the day he visits us' (*I Peter 2:12*). Note the use of the word 'see' in *I Peter 2:12*. This is the opposite of hearing you tell them all about the good deeds you may have done.

The above scriptures teach us that it is God's will for all christians to have a good reputation with the unbelieving world.

A man or woman in a spiritual leadership position who has a bad reputation with those outside the church is likely to bring disgrace to the name of Jesus Christ and the local church. This bad reputation is likely to lead to criticism and hinder the work of God in the local area.

I knew a church pastor who told me when he arrived at a small town, he discovered that the previous pastor had many outstanding bills and a zero-credit rating with local businesses. The church had a reputation for not paying its bills, and when asked about overdue payments, the previous pastor always considered this as persecution by the ungodly. The church had a bad name, was losing people, and the name of Jesus Christ was treated with contempt in the local business community. The pastor and the church had a bad reputation with those outside and a great blockage to wining people for the Lord. That local church became a disgrace in the local community and had fallen into the devil's trap.

> If a person who has a bad reputation with unbelievers is appointed to a spiritual leadership position, it creates problems for the body of Christ, and for the church leader.

Criticism of the spiritual leader because of their bad reputation may lead to the leader becoming focused on themselves, having a 'pity party' attitude to life, rather than on God's work. They may become depressed or disillusioned with church life and resign their position or move on to a leadership role in another church. The devil's trap has claimed another victim. If the underlying cause of the person's bad reputation has not been dealt with, this destructive cycle may be repeated.

You should not be surprised when you are criticised by unbelievers for something when you did not deserve it (*I John 3:13*). Since the world hated Jesus, we should not be surprised when people who do not know God hate us also (*John 15:18 - 20*). I believe that if everything is going smoothly, everyone loves you and there is no one who opposes you or hates you or what you stand for, then you should be careful and examine your own life. If unjust criticism is not happening to you now, it soon will, I can guarantee it, provided you are living as you should (*Luke 6:26*).

After reminding christians it is blessed to be reviled for the name of Christ, Peter warns us '*If you suffer, it should not be as a murder, thief, or any other kind of criminal, or even as a meddler.*' (*I Peter 4:15*) Though criticism from unbelievers often accompanies a godly lifestyle, it should never result from ungodly behaviour.

How should you react when people falsely or unjustly criticise you ?

'*Opponents must be gently instructed, in the hope that God will grant them repentance leading them to a knowledge of the truth, and that they will come to their senses and escape from the trap of the devil, who has taken them captive to do his will.*' (*II Timothy 2:25, 26*). Paul is teaching us that our reactions when someone criticizes us should be restrained in the hope that God will grant that person (or people) repentance. This is often hard for most of us in a church leadership position and can only be achieved as we live day by day in His grace.

Never give up or despair if you are being criticised by unbelievers, even if it is for something wrong you have done. Remember in the Old Testament even Abraham and his son Isaac were criticised for telling lies to save themselves, by saying that their wives were their sisters. In fact, both lied to the same ungodly man (*Genesis 20:1 - 17* and *26:7 - 11*). Peter encourages the christians who are being criticised for righteousness' sake to take heart and not to feel guilty or embarrassed (*I Peter 4:15, 16*).

God is compassionate and He asks that we should be also, especially on those who have fallen into the trap of the devil (*Isaiah 40:1, 2* ; *James 5:11* and *19, 20*). Paul wrote to the Corinthians urging them to restore the one they had disciplined, lest he be '*overwhelmed by excessive sorrow*' (*II Corinthians 2:7*). Note that this man was sinning more than was even approved by unbelievers (*I Corinthians 5:1*). Yet Paul showed the compassion of God even on this man.

It is important to note that to fail as a spiritual leader and be criticised by unbelievers for bad behaviour is also to fail other members of the body of Christ. Don't, Paul taught, put a man or woman with this kind of spiritual immaturity in a position of spiritual leadership, for they will surely fall into the devil's trap when criticised by unbelievers.

Personal application

The following personal application is designed to help you develop a good reputation with unbelievers.

➢ Read again the scripture passages and discussion above. Think about the example of a pastor and church with a bad reputation for not paying its bills.

➢ Answering the following questions may help you to test if you have a good reputation with those outside of the kingdom of God. Be honest! How do you measure up ? Find the verses of scripture from those given above (or others that God may show you) that are relevant to answering each question.

1)   Do I live my life in a wise way, regarding both my speech and my general conduct ?

People who are not christian should be happy to talk to you without being 'put-off' by your general attitude, speech, or spiritualization of every situation. Can you share about your experiences with God in a non-threatening manner ? Jesus talked to and spent time with those that were looked down upon by the religious people of the day (for example *Luke 5:30*). You and I should do the same today.

2)   Am I above criticism regarding my attitude to paying my bills ?

If you can't pay your bills on time, ring up, explain, and organise an extension or time payments. Most business understand and are willing to delay payment or make other arrangements if asked before the due date.

This shows you are willing to pay but are honest and having financial difficulties. If you follow through on your commitments, you will gain a good reputation.

3)   Is my social life a good testimony before unbelievers ?

This includes social media accounts. There have been instances where people have lost their jobs because of what they posted on-line. It also includes how you behave in public with your spouse and family and your attitude to alcohol, gambling and inappropriate jokes or rumours at work or your neighbourhood.

4)   Do I show respect to my employer, boss, employees, friends, relatives and neighbours ? Read again *Ephesian 6:5 - 9*.

5)   Do I live a consistent and exemplary life, even when I am falsely accused ?

Take specific steps of action in areas of your life where you are weak. The following questions that may help you do this.

➢ Have you made amends for your wrong behaviour toward unbelievers, particularly when it has hurt the body of Christ ?

➢ Is an apology necessary to your family or relatives, your unsaved neighbour, your employer, or employees ?

➢ What goals do you need to set up regarding your future behaviour ?

Life Quality Number 15 -
Not pursuing dishonest gain

'*Since an overseer manages God's household, he must be blameless - not overbearing, not overbearing, not quick-tempered, not given to drunkenness, not violent, **not pursuing dishonest gain.**' (**Titus 1:7**)*

'*Not a lover of money*' is discussed as a separate life quality, number 11, as this refers to valuing money or material possessions above God and eternal treasures, rather than the methods of obtaining these things.

'*Not pursuing dishonest gain*' refers to wrong or dishonest accumulation of wealth. It may involve deliberate deception regarding selling your car, your house, your computer, or anything else you own. God expects all christians to be honest and fair in their financial dealings.

'*Use honest scales and honest weights, an honest ephah and an honest hin. I am the Lord your God, who brought you out of Egypt.*' **Leviticus 19:36**

'*The Lord detests dishonest scales, but accurate weights find favour with him.*' **Proverbs 11:1**

Similar words can be found in **Proverbs 20:23** and **Ezekiel 45:10**.

God tells the prophet Amos that he will spare his people no longer for having dishonest scales and boosting the price of merchandise (for excessive profit) (**Amos 8:1 - 6**). Similar words were written by the prophet Micah (**Micah 6:9 – 16**). James teaches us that riches gained by dishonest means (including 'ripping people off' or withholding fair wages due for your employees) will cry against people in eternity (**James 5:1 - 6**).

What we do with our finances, including deliberately overcharging customers in the business world, or being dishonest in our dealings with our everyday activities, with insurance or Centrelink claims, must be weighed against Gods' standards.

Once I was shopping when the lady at the checkout gave me change from a $50 note, when I had I had only given her a $20 note. When I realised and tried to give the money back, the lady at the check-out said, "Thank for your honesty, sir, God bless you".

Many people will make a scene or complain if they are overcharged or short-changed at the supermarket or shop, but we as mature christians need to put things right when we are under-charged just as much as when we are over-changed.

Some of us think of businesses who may have cheated customers by charging higher prices than they should or corporate tax cheats who may have defrauded the tax office by keeping dishonest records. However, what about you and me when it comes to income tax returns or services from trades people ?

On more than one occasion, I have had a trades person who had a cash only price quote which was much cheaper than the book price when quoting for some work for me. (The cash only price was when the job was to be done 'off the books', with no record of income or tax paid, which is completely dishonest). I always insist on the book price.

I said to one such tradesman, "I want the book price because doing a job for cash is simply dishonest." He said to me, "God bless you brother because if the job is not done 'on the books' then I can't come back and fix or repair anything that goes wrong." There is no guarantee for work that is done without a proper record, which includes income received and tax paid.

An accountant who organised my tax return once told me that the amount of the return I can get you is dependent on how much you are prepared to lie, because the Government will never check up on your claimed expenses in certain areas if you keep them below a certain limit. He was shocked when I said no, even more so when I said this was dishonest and I can't do that and still claim to serve God.

If we are trying to get done things done or buy things 'on the cheap' or finding or participating in ways to accumulate wealth by avoiding tax or paying others less than we rightfully have to, then we are pursuing dishonest gain. In doing so, we send the message to those who do not know the Lord as we do, that money is more important to us than God.

God provides for you, and He will make sure you have what you need as a father provides for his children, even before we ask Him (*Mathew 6:8* and *33, 34*; *Mathew 7:11* and *Luke 11:13*).

A mature christian will have this faith in God demonstrated in his or her daily life, attitudes to his pay-packet or other income source, bills and expenses, and conversations.

Personal application

The following personal application is designed to help you avoid pursuing dishonest gain. Evaluate your attitude towards money. Answer these questions as honestly as you can.

➢ Am I honest about my tax return ?

➢ What is my reaction when I am asked to join a legally right money-making scheme that may be morally questionable ?

➢ When I am short-changed at the shop, do I react the same as when I receive more change than I should ?

➢ What personal steps do I need to take in these areas to avoid pursuing dishonest gain ?

Life Quality Number 16 -
Keep hold of the deep truths of the faith with a clear conscience

'*They must **keep hold of the deep truths of the faith with a clear conscience**' (I Timothy 3:9*)

'*He must hold firmly to the trustworthy message as it has been taught, so that he can encourage others by sound doctrine and refute those who oppose it.*' (**Titus 1:9**)

This life quality is about learning and understanding the deep truths of the Word of God.

'*Brothers and sisters, I could not address you as people who live by the Spirit but as people who are still worldly - mere infants in Christ. I gave you milk, not solid food, for you were not yet ready for it. Indeed, you are still not ready. You are still worldly. For since there is jealousy and quarrelling among you, are you not worldly ? Are you not acting like mere humans ? For when one says, "I follow Paul," and another, "I follow Apollos," are you not mere human beings ?*' (**I Corinthians 3:1 – 4**)

Most people would think it very unusual or there was something very wrong with a teenager or young adult eating baby food, drinking milk out of a baby's bottle, or still wearing nappies (or diapers). That is what Paul emphasized was a problem with the people in Corinth (read the verse above). Paul also points out a similar problem in the book of Hebrews (**Hebrews 5: 12 – 6:3**).

If you are still being taught or only know about the elementary truths of God's Word, such as repentance from sin, resurrection of the dead and eternal judgement, then you are still a baby in Christ and not mature enough in your knowledge of God's Word to be a spiritual leader in God's house.

> A mature man or woman of God understands there is more to the christian life than living to enter heaven and avoid hell. His or her knowledge of God's Word is more than the basics needed for fire insurance.

Mature christian people have grown in understanding the Bible and their relationship with Jesus Christ, how to live by faith in all areas of life, how to know, follow and be obedient to God's small voice, and how to share their christian life with others in a non-threatening way. The only way to grow in these areas of life is by '*constant use to train themselves*' or by exercising their faith and trust in God (*Hebrews 5:12 - 14*). And that takes discipline, courage, and time.

If your relationship with God is shallow you can only lead other people in shallow teachings, and you will find it difficult to relate to or lead others when they face the crises of life. You will likely have limited material of your own to teach people about living for God. Some will soon realise how shallow you are in your christian life and may leave the church to find someone else who will teach them.

If people can't see your christian character in your everyday life, then they will not be drawn to the God you serve. They will be turned off and may conclude the christian life is nothing more than a set of rules or about doing what I say and not what I do.

Note that this life quality is about understanding God's Word with a clear conscience. You can only have a clear conscience if you are applying what you learn to your own life and obeying what God has taught you and told you to do. If God has convicted you to change something in your life, then please do it in obedience to Him. Disobedience will destroy or sear your clear conscience like a hot iron (*I Timothy 4:1 – 3*). You cannot expect God to teach you more if you are not putting into practice what He has already shown you and you have learnt from Him.

Don't feel condemned if there are areas of your life that you still struggle with, even though God is dealing with you through what you have learnt from this Bible teaching series so far. We all have struggles and weakness; it is what you do with these areas of your life that counts.

Remember the devil comes to steal, kill, and destroy your christian life (*John 10:10*). His best weapon is to discourage you to try to make you give up or complain because of your feelings (*Numbers 21:4, 5*). The devil comes to condemn and discourage you, but God comes to convict and forgive you (*John 16:8 ; I John 1:9*).

Paul teaches us in *Titus chapter 1* that there are two reasons why a mature christian person needs to understand the deep truths of God's Word. Firstly, so that you can encourage others by teaching sound doctrine, and secondly so that you can refute those who oppose the teaching of God's Word.

A mature man or woman of God recognises that God's Word is the only truth and ultimate authority in their life and ministry. Church doctrine or religious practices, leadership principles based more on the worldly ways than Godly ways, or personal views on theology, ultimately do not encourage or inspire others to follow God for themselves. Relying on such things is likely to result in arguments. Arguments, including justifications of personal religious theories, will never win anyone to Christ, as that is the job of the Holy Spirit and His alone (*John 16:7 – 11*)

It is one thing to love God, and to love and know His Word, but a mature christian person has leant to apply the scriptures in a wise and understanding way. '*For this reason, since the day we heard about you, we have not stopped praying for you. We continually ask God to fill you with the knowledge of his will through all the wisdom and understanding that the Spirit gives, so that you may live a life worthy of the Lord and please him in every way: bearing fruit in every good work, growing in the knowledge of God,*' (*Colossians 1:9, 10*).

Prayer is the key that unlocks the Word of God and opens our eyes and our hearts to the voice of the Spirit of God. He enables us to know how to apply the Word of God to our lives in a wise and understanding way.

Personal application

The following personal application is designed to help you grow in your knowledge of the deep truths of God's Word.

> - Carefully study *I Timothy chapter 4*. Right down what you learn from this chapter about those who have their conscience seared. Do you discover anything about issues you should avoid and items you should teach ? Write your discoveries down. Make it your goal to apply what you learn from this chapter to your daily life and ministry.

> - Honestly evaluate your life to determine if there are areas where you have learnt from God but have not applied what you have learnt to your personal life. Take practical steps to enable this application to your life to occur.

> - Please, do not procrastinate.

> - Do your best to improve the quality of your own quite time with God. Take notes on paper or electronically of what God shows you from His Word. Ensure you are obedient to His still small voice as much as you possibly can.

> - Join or enrol in Bible teaching classes or courses.

> - Take notes while listening to sermons at church to understand all that was said or obtain and watch CDs or internet downloads of church sermons.

> - Read books or watch internet downloads of christian teaching, or life stories of great heroes of the faith from now and in times past.

> - Volunteer to assist in teaching Bible classes or in church activities.

Life Quality Number 17 -
Not overbearing

'*Since an overseer manages God's household, he must be blameless - **not overbearing**'* (*Titus 1:7*)

The Greek word '*authadés*' translated as '*overbearing*' has a literal English meaning of '*self-satisfied, self-pleasing, arrogant, stubborn*'[24]. This Greek word appears in only one other verse in the New Testament, **II Peter chapter 2** [25], where it is referring to false teachers. Such people '*follow the corrupt desire of the flesh and despise authority*' and are '*bold and **arrogant***' (*verse 10*) (emphasis added to the original text to highlight the same Greek word for overbearing as in **Titus 1:7**).

Peter explains in the rest of this chapter, that these false teachers '*blaspheme in matters they do not understand*' (*verse 12*), are '*blots and blemishes ... while they feast with you*' (*verse 13*) and have '*eyes full of adultery*' (*verse 14*). These people '*mouth empty, boastful words ... entice people who are just escaping ... they promise them freedom while they themselves are slaves of depravity*' (*verses 18* and *19*).

An overbearing person is arrogant and self-centred with a 'I will do as I please' attitude to life, with no thought or concern as to how this behaviour or attitude affects others.

A christian person who is overbearing often lives a life of pious behaviour with ' holier than thou ' attitudes judging the behaviour of others. They usually rationalise their behaviour on some biblical grounds taken completely out of context and refuse correction by anyone, including those in authority over them, and sadly often even by God himself.

---

24 - *Greek word and meaning from Strong's Concordance*

25 - *Thayer (1979)*

In a spiritual leadership role, an overbearing person often becomes one who shepherds the flock of God by constantly dominating or lording over those entrusted to them.

A Pastor of a local church I was attending very quickly asserted his authority in the Lord on any matter in the church. Anyone who dared to question him was soon told he was questioning the 'Word of the Lord'. No one could suggest anything or have any word from God other than what he agreed with first. That church had major problems, financially and spiritually and endured numerous church splits, which was devastating to the work of the Lord in the general area. Eventually, God had to remove this man due to ill - health before His work could proceed.

Anyone such as this pastor who thinks they always know best can become a spiritual 'know - it - all' who cannot accept or is threatened by challenge or change. Such a person has the attitude that they are perfect here on earth. Some modern-day examples of overbearing people:

- James has a wife and two teen-age children. Sure, he is a christian, and he even gets his family to church every Sunday, and mostly on time. He has family devotions most days and is a good provider for them both, has a steady, well-paid job and will always defend his family. To all outside observers, he is a good christian family man. His wife and children, however, will tell you he runs his home like a dictator. He makes all the decisions. They have no choice or say about anything. He rules the family with an iron fist. It is always simply his way or no way. He would never think of compromise for the sake of other family members.

- John works in a local factory. As far as his work goes, he never misses a day for no reason, does his job well and is an exceptionally good and faithful employee. His nickname behind his back, however, is 'Mr. perfect'. "He thinks he's never wrong!" say his fellow employees. He will never admit he has made a mistake, says his boss, even when everybody else knows he has.

- Henry is on the church board. He always finds reasons why an idea will not work or complains about its cost. The only time that he agrees with an idea is when he suggested it in the first place. Ideas or suggestions from other board members just can never match his own 'holy ghost inspired' suggestions.

James, John, and Henry all exhibit behavioural patterns consistent with having an overbearing personality. If (or in the case of Henry when) any of these men are appointed in church leadership positions, their self-will will create major problems for the local church.

Any man or woman who has exhibits overbearing behaviour, such as in the examples above, needs to face themselves realistically and, by God's grace, overcome the problem if they want to take on a spiritual leadership role. How do you do this ? Some of the answers can be found in the following personal application.

Personal application

The following personal application is designed to help you determine if you are an overbearing person and help you overcome such behavioural patterns.

- ➤ Study the following Bible verses to learn how you should treat other christian people - *Matthew 25:31 – 46* and *Ephesians chapter 4*.

- ➤ If you are overbearing because you have always been allowed to get your own way, then stop acting that way! It is really that simple. It is your choice!

- ➤ Allow Jesus Christ to control you.

- ➤ Find out what the Bible teaches about being a gracious, loving, and unselfish christian and then start loving people. For example - *I Peter 3 : 8 – 14*

- ➤ Stop using people for your own ends.

- ➤ Allow the Holy Spirit through the Word of God to produce His fruit in your life. Read *Galatians 5:22 - 26* and ask God to show you how to better live this kind of life than you are now.

However, if your problem is difficult for you to understand, you may need some professional help from a competent christian counsellor. You may need someone who can help you understand why the problem exists, and then help you to set up goals for overcoming the problem.

Warning: Frequently people who have problems of being over-bearing tend to rationalise their behaviour once they understand why they are the way they are. Over-bearing people often continue to live irresponsible lives, going on in their sin, while at the same time blaming someone else for creating their problems. (Read *James 1:13 – 15*).

Remember: God holds all of us responsible for our own actions, no matter what the cause of the problems. He understands and sympathises, but we must begin to act responsibly through the resources that He gives us. (Read *James chapter 4*).

Life Quality Number 18 - Must love what is good

'*Rather, he must be hospitable, **one who loves what is good***'. (***Titus 1:8***)

We are not to '*be overcome by evil*'. Instead, Paul teaches that we are to '*overcome evil with good*' (***Romans 12:21***). How do you overcome evil with good ?

Paul makes it clear how you '*will be able to test and approve what God's will is – his good, pleasing and perfect will.*' (***Romans 12:1, 2***). You must present your bodies as a living and holy sacrifice. A sacrifice has no rights of its own; imagine the goat getting up of the altar as the knife comes down!

You must not be conformed to this world, but be transformed by the renewing of your mind, which is an act of your will. This involves a determined effort on your part. God doesn't demand it or do this for us, but He urges us to do it for ourselves, (often even begs us to do it). His appeal is based on what He has done for us, which is His marvellous grace or His mercy, which was given to us through His Son Jesus Christ (***Romans 12:1***).

'*Finally, brothers and sisters, whatever is true, whatever is noble, whatever is right, whatever is pure, whatever is lovely, whatever is admirable - if anything is excellent or praiseworthy - think about such things*' (***Philippians 4:8***).

This scripture should govern what we allow and refuse to allow ourselves to think about another person. It provides a good test to see if you really look for the good in someone else (no matter what they may have done to you first).

You must understand that this is your choice; it is your will governing what you think about another person.

> Someone who loves what is good desires to do good for other people and to think about the good in them rather than the evil.

Paul also teaches us in **Ephesians 4:29** *'Do not let any unwholesome talk come out of your mouths, but only what is helpful for building others up according to their needs,'*.

'To the pure, all things are pure, but to those who are corrupted and do not believe, nothing is pure. In fact, both their minds and consciences are corrupted. They claim to know God, but by their actions they deny him. They are detestable, disobedient and unfit for doing anything good.' (**Titus 1:15, 16**)

Jesus stated that the Pharisees do good only to those who they expect to do good to them in return, but we as His disciples should do good to all men, regardless of whether or not they do good or evil to us (**Matthew 5:43 – 47**). The Pharisees according to Jesus receive a reward for their good works here on earth, with no reward in heaven (**Mathew 6:16 – 18**). That is the reason for Jesus' teaching about turning the other cheek or going the extra mile (doing more than the minimum legally required) (**Matthew 5:38 – 42**).

A mature christian person who learns to love what is good must first be someone who loves God, for God is good. He or she must strive to give everything over to God and desire to walk consistently day by day in His will. This can only happen as a person grows in the knowledge of God's Word and applies it to their life (**Matthew 7:24 - 27**).

Doing good for others must be based on God's love. '*We love because he first loved us. Whoever claims to love God yet hates a brother or sister is a liar. For whoever does not love their brother and sister, whom they have seen, cannot love God, whom they have not seen. And he has given us this command: Anyone who loves God must also love their brother and sister.*' (**I John 4:19 - 21**).

We do good to others because God has been good to us, not with any ulterior motive such as to win them for the Lord. Our motive must be love so that we show them God's love. This will result in a reward in heaven, not an earthly reward.

It is difficult for most of us to walk in or do good to others as consistently as we should, due to our fallen nature inherited from Adam and Eve. It is only as we determine to '*do good to all men*' (**Galatians 6:10**), and then draw upon God's resources, that we will be able to act towards other people the way we should. Developing this desire to love good and hate evil is part of the process of becoming mature or becoming more like Jesus Christ.

Paul wrote to Timothy to urge him to continue to practice doing good in his life; to continue in the things he has learned and become convinced of (**II Timothy 3:14**). He was referring, of course, to the Holy scriptures, which are '*useful for teaching, rebuking, correcting and training in righteousness; that the servant of God may be thoroughly equipped for every good work.*' (**II Timothy 3:15 – 17**).

To 'love what is good' is more than thought, it is an action. It is something we strive to do every day. '*For we must all appear before the judgment seat of Christ, so that each of us may receive what is due us for the things done while in the body, whether good or bad.*' (**II Corinthians 5:10.**)

Personal application

This personal application is designed to help you love what is good. Evaluate your daily actions and motivations by Scriptural standards. Are you practicing the following Biblical directives in your daily life ?

> ➢ Do I take advantage of all opportunities to do good to all men, those who are christian and those who are not, regardless of race, skin colour or social standing ? Read *Galatians 6:10* and *Titus 3:1, 2*.

> ➢ Do I have a good conscience regarding my behaviour ? Read *I Timothy 1:18, 19*.

> ➢ Am I using my material resources to help others in need ? Read *II Corinthians 9:6 – 8*.

> ➢ Do I build people up or do I tear them down ? Read *Ephesians 4:29*.

Now that you have done your part, trust God to do His. Claim the following promises for your own life from God's Word:

'being confident of this, that he who began a good work in you will carry it on to completion until the day of Christ Jesus.' (*Philippians 1:6*).

'Now may the God of peace, who through the blood of the eternal covenant brought back from the dead our Lord Jesus, that great Shepherd of the sheep, equip you with everything good for doing his will, and may he work in us what is pleasing to him, through Jesus Christ, to whom be glory for ever and ever. Amen.' (*Hebrews 13:20, 21*).

146

Life Quality Number 19 - Upright

'*Rather, he must be hospitable, one who loves what is good, **upright**, holy*' (*Titus 1:8*)

For most of us, upright and holy are two words in the English language that mean essentially the same thing - living a life that is honest, holy, just (or prudent) by doing the right thing both ethically and morally. Both English words imply living a life trying to do more of the right things than the wrong things, even when other people are not watching or when doing so may result in the loss of friends, popularity, or money.

In *Titus 1:8*, Paul deliberately uses two different Greek words which are translated as the English words '*upright*' and '*holy*'. He uses a common Greek word '*dikaios*' which is translated as 'upright'. In the context of this verse, it has a literal English meaning of '*rendering to each his due in a judicial sense, passing just judgement on others, whether in expressed in words or shown by the manner of dealing with them*'. However, Paul uses the Greek word '*hosios*' which is translated as '*holy*', which has a literal English meaning of '*being undefiled by sin, free from wickedness, religiously observing every moral obligation, pure holy, pious*'[26].

In this book, '*upright*' and '*holy*' are discussed as two separate life qualities, due to the differences between these two words in the Greek text.

Paul defines for us how to live an upright life in the following verses.

---

26 - Both Greek words and meaning from Strong's Concordance

'*I urge, then, first of all, that petitions, prayers, intercession and thanksgiving be made for all people, for kings and all those in authority, that we may live peaceful and quiet lives in all godliness and holiness. This is good, and pleases God our Saviour, who wants all people to be saved and to come to a knowledge of the truth.*' (*I Timothy 2:1 – 4*).

'*Let everyone be subject to the governing authorities, for there is no authority except that which God has established. The authorities that exist have been established by God. Consequently, whoever rebels against the authority is rebelling against what God has instituted, and those who do so will bring judgment on themselves.*

For rulers hold no terror for those who do right, but for those who do wrong. Do you want to be free from fear of the one in authority? Then do what is right and you will be commended. For the one in authority is God's servant for your good. But if you do wrong, be afraid, for rulers do not bear the sword for no reason. They are God's servants, agents of wrath to bring punishment on the wrongdoer. Therefore, it is necessary to submit to the authorities, not only because of possible punishment but also as a matter of conscience.' (*Romans 13:1 – 5*)

'*Slaves, obey your earthly masters with respect and fear, and with sincerity of heart, just as you would obey Christ. Obey them not only to win their favour when their eye is on you, but as slaves of Christ, doing the will of God from your heart*' (*Ephesians 6:5, 6*). Paul gives similar teaching in (*Colossians 3:22 – 25*).

'*Do everything without grumbling or arguing, so that you may become blameless and pure, children of God without fault in a warped and crooked generation.*' (*Philippians 2:14, 15*).

> Our reactions and actions should reflect an upright life in every situation we face in our daily lives.

Think about the following four everyday life situations

1)   Your daily prayer life.

❑ Do you deliberately pray for the leaders and those who rule over you in your daily prayer life before God ? Remember if you pray this way it pleases God, which should be your number one priority. These leaders include:

❑ Our government leaders – Federal, State and Local, even if you don't like the political party or group they represent.

❑ Our bosses at work – even if you don't like what they do or their attitude towards you or other employees.

❑ The police that you may see on the roads.

❑ Our church leaders – even if you have difficulties with accepting some of their decisions.

2)   Your reactions to your bosses or leaders.

❑ If you are complaining about your boss behind his or her back like everybody else, you are not living an upright life.

❑ If you consistently arrive a few minutes late to work or cut for home a few minutes early, cheat on your timesheet even it is only by a few minutes, waste work time by prolonged idle talk, excessive coffee breaks or any other means, or take things home to keep or use at home when not authorised or you do not have permission to do so, you are not living the upright life God expects you to.

3)   Your attitude to the laws of the land.

❑ If you are caught speeding by the policeman, policewoman or the speed camera, you are receiving a just reward for not living an upright life.

❑ When you park illegally at the shopping centre or anywhere else, even if you are in the disabled parking area only for a minute while you quickly go to the ATM or the shop for one or two things, you are not obeying the laws of the land.

❑ If you deliberately go through the yellow traffic light when you had time to stop, don't stop at a stop sign, don't obey the speed rules, or cut someone else off as you speed past, you are not living the upright life God asks you to live.

4)   Honouring those to whom honour is due.

- ❏ You should pay respect or honour to those to whom it is due, even if you do not agree with what the person may do or their reputation, or do not particularly like what they represent. When you fail to honour someone, from a politician to a sporting hero or a person who has gained a recognition for what they have achieved, then you are not living an upright life. This applies to the position a person may hold in society, rather than the person themselves. *'Give to everyone what you owe them: If you owe taxes, pay taxes; if revenue, then revenue; if respect, then respect; if honor, then honor.'* (**Romans 13:7**).

Personal application

The following personal application is designed to help you live an upright life.

➢ Review the four life situations above about how living an upright life should be shown in your everyday life situations. How do you rate yourself in each of these ? Be as honest as you can as you think about your reactions in each of these situations.

➢ Make an action plan to try to improve in any of these that you may identify where you need improving. For example, if you know you should improve your personal prayer life by praying for your leaders and rulers over you, then make a list and have it with you when you pray. If find yourself complaining like everybody else, then ask God to help you change and say something positive about your boss when others are being negative.

➢ Implement your action plan and see yourself improve in living an upright life before God and others.

Life Quality Number 20 - Holy

'*Rather he must be hospitable, one who loves what is good, who is self-controlled, **upright,** **holy**' (**Titus 1:8**).

God calls us to be holy, or to live a holy life. '*For God did not call us to be impure, but to live a holy life. Therefore, anyone who rejects this instruction does not reject a human being but God, the very God who gives you his Holy Spirit..*' (**I Thessalonians 4:7 – 8**)

> Holiness refers to a way of life, or a lifestyle as an individual christian daily living before God.

I Peter 2:9, 10 teaches us everyone who is born again is part of a chosen people, a royal priesthood, a holy nation, and God's special possession. This is a holiness because of who you are and what Jesus Christ has done for you (sometimes called positional holiness). It has nothing to do with what you do or do not do (nothing to do with keeping or not keeping the rules) and is different to the holiness referred to in **Titus chapter 1**. You are holy because you are saved by the blood of Jesus Christ.

However, you should also live a holy life (to the best of your ability) because that is what God has commanded you to do (**I Peter 1:13 – 16, Leviticus 11:44, 45** and **19:2**).

Confusing these two aspects of holiness can lead to incorrect teaching regarding Biblical holiness.

Some wrong concepts or thinking about being 'holy'.

1) <u>You as a christian are automatically holy without any thought regarding how you live your daily lives</u> (quoting verses such as *I Peter 2:9, 10*).

This interpretation of the word 'holy' is incorrect as not one of us can be holy before God all the time. Bible verses such as **Romans 3:23** ('*For all have sinned*') show us that this interpretation of the meaning of holiness is inconsistent with Biblical teaching. The children of Israel, who were God's chosen and holy people, were often called upon by the Old Testament prophets to repent of their ways and return to the Lord their God.

Too many christian people do terrible and evil things in their life because of this erroneous teaching, which leads to the charge of being hypocritical or a 'do as I say, not as I do' attitude. This teaching also ignores other Bible verses, such as *I John 1:9*. Read **Psalm 90** for a reference to remember regarding God judging His people.

2) <u>Holiness equals being separated from the world or sinners</u>.

Bible verses such as **Hebrews 7:26** and **II Corinthians 6:17, 18** are used by some people to justify this wrong thinking. However, other verses such as *John 17:15 - 19 ; I Corinthians 5:9, 10* and *Matthew 5:13 -16* should also be considered in interpretation of what holiness is. These verses teach us that God's intention is not to take us out of the world. We should be part of the world; seasoning the world as salt seasons, flavours, or preserves our food.

3) <u>Some religions today teach that to be holy means to be ceremonially washed from the contamination of the world,</u> for example by cleansing your face and hands using a special cloth before eating.

This teaching is similar to the teaching of the pharisees of Jesus day. Jesus had no hesitation rebuking the pharisees for having such a religious attitude toward holiness. Read verses such as *Mark 7:1 – 23* and *Luke 11:37 - 53.*

4) <u>Holiness equals not sinning</u>.

If this were the case, we could never be holy, because we all fall short of God's glory (*Romans 3:23*). Verses such as *I John 1:9* would not be needed. A holy life should be free from known sin and from unknown sin as much as possible.

5) <u>Holiness equals keeping a set of man-made rules</u>.

This is what the pharisees and other religious leaders taught in Jesus' day.

In *Matthew 15:1 - 20* Jesus said that the pharisees nullify the Word of God because their religious rules (their traditions) were based on rules taught by men. Paul shows us in *Colossians 2:20 - 23* that to keep man-made rules does not make you holy (help you restrain sensual indulgence).

So, what is a holy life ?

How can a holy life be seen or demonstrated ? Is God calling us to be something that we are not or can never be ? Paul in *Ephesians chapters 4, 5* and *6* answers these questions and gives us criteria to evaluate the holiness of our own life from God's perspective.

Chapter 4

- ➢ v 20   Holiness is learned behaviour
- ➢ v 22-24   You can change from unholy to holy behaviour
- ➢ v25   Laying aside all falsehood
- ➢ v26   Laying aside all wrongful anger
- ➢ v28   Laying aside stealing
- ➢ v29   No unwholesome talk or jokes (also *chapter 5:4*)
- ➢ v30   Not grieving the Holy Spirit
- ➢ v32   Being kind, compassionate and forgiving

Chapter 5

- ➢ v2   Loving
- ➢ v3   No sexual immorality, impurity, or greed
- ➢ v8, 9   Walking as children of the light
- ➢ v11   Exposing deeds of darkness
- ➢ v18   Not getting drunk
- ➢ v21   Being subject to each other
- ➢ v 25 – 33   Husbands and wives treating each other well

> ➤ v1   Obedient children
> ➤ v4   Being Godly fathers
> ➤ v5   Working hard and honestly
> ➤ v9   Not treating harshly those you employ, or are the
>   boss of at work

I believe holiness is living a life that is both morally and legally right, because there is a difference. Jesus was angry with the Pharisees of his day, because they were so concentrated on doing everything exactly right according to the letter of the law they were blind to the life that the Spirit of God offered them.

'He has made us competent as ministers of a new covenant - not of the letter but of the Spirit; for the letter kills, but the Spirit gives life.' (**II Corinthians 3:6**).

'Woe to you, teachers of the law and Pharisees, you hypocrites! You give a tenth of your spices - mint, dill and cumin. But you have neglected the more important matters of the law - justice, mercy and faithfulness. You should have practiced the latter, without neglecting the former. You blind guides! You strain out a gnat but swallow a camel.' (**Matthew 23:23, 24**).

Some christian people in our day can have a similar attitude by being so concerned with not doing the don'ts (the man-made rules to define what a holy life is) that they don't have time to do the dos. The don'ts are often rules made by men. Keeping such man-made rules will not make you holy in God's eyes (**Colossians 2:20 – 23**).

Paul also shows us that holiness is more than just outward actions. Holiness also involves our thought patterns. Read *Philippians 4:8*. If your thought patterns are based on what Paul defines in this verse, negative thoughts, gossip, criticisms, unhealthy desires, and emotions, and often stomach ulcers, should become patterns of the life you used to live, and not of your new life in Christ.

Personal application

The following personal application is designed to help you develop the quality of holiness in your life.

> ➤ The verses from Paul's letter to the Ephesians listed above describe practical holiness in daily living. Use the list as criteria for determining areas in your own life that need improvement.

> ➤ Make each one you that you noted a personal goal in your own life. Be specific in your goal setting based on your own set of circumstances and your own needs.

> ➤ As you learn to develop these goals in your daily life, you will be growing in the holy life that God expects you to live.

Life Quality Number 21 - Disciplined

'*Rather he must be hospitable, one who loves what is good, who is self-controlled, upright, holy and **disciplined**.*' (***Titus 1:8***)

When I look through the books on sale at a christian bookshop it is hard to find a book entitled 'The benefits of Christian Discipline' or 'Christian Discipline'. The topic is certainly not as popular today as such topics as The Holy Spirit, The Anointing, Christian Victory, Angels and Demons, Spiritual Gifts, Claiming your destiny or healing, God's end time calendar, or series of sermons, tapes or videos from the latest church conference or "hot" preacher.

Why ? Because I believe that most christian people do not wish to know about christian discipline. It is simply not popular to talk about the subject. If you do talk about it, immediately many people will cry "Legalism" or "We have been set free from the law."

Others will tell you they tried but failed, "it is just too hard", or "it just does not fit into a modern lifestyle" or the "new agenda of the 21st century church". "Don't talk or preach about that brother; it brings me into condemnation which is not what a church minister is supposed to do". Yet these people forget or deliberately ignore that living a christian life according to Biblical standards requires sacrifice and discipline.

> I believe God's Spirit will judge the church if we allow the lawlessness of the world to creep into our christian thinking or teaching by becoming undisciplined in our christian life.

"Do your own thing" or "We have been set free by the blood of Jesus" we are told by some christian churches. Those who promote such ideas I believe have failed to consult the Word of God to see what God has to say regarding discipline.

Christian discipline is **NOT** legalism. *Colossians chapter 2* is often used to argue that we are free from christian laws about how to live and free from christian discipline. Verses 16 to 23 of this chapter are often used by people who argue that any form of laws for a christian is 'Legalism'. However, these people fail to read the next chapter of Colossians (*chapter 3:1 - 11*) where Paul teaches us to look above and live for heavenly principles and rewards and not for earthly gain or pleasure.

The key to understanding *Colossians chapter 2* is found in *verse 22*, '*These rules, which have to do with things that are all destined to perish with use, are based on merely human commands and teachings.*' If the commands to not touch, taste or be involved with come from men and not from God they are legalistic and clearly wrong !

There are rules for christian living that we should obey, which we can read in some of Paul's letters, (*Ephesians 5:15 – 6:9 ; Colossians 3:18 - 25;* and *Titus 3:1 – 11*). We are commanded by Paul not to use our freedom to cause someone else to stumble in his or her christian life (*Romans 14:13 - 23*, particularly *verses 19 – 21*).

Paul declared that though he was free because of what Christ has done for him, he would never use this freedom to indulge in his sinful nature (*Galatians 5:13 - 15*). Similarly, Peter commands us never to use our freedom as a cover-up or justification for evil (*I Peter 2:16*)

The Bible is very clear that mature christian people have trained themselves by discipline to discern good and evil (*Hebrews 5:11 – 14*). The only way to become the mature man or woman of God that He intended you to be is to develop and maintain a disciplined christian life, in terms of prayer times, bible reading times and listening to and obeying the voice of the Holy Spirit. Undisciplined christians are still babes in Christ, feeding on the milk of the God's Word.

There are three illustrations of disciplined people found in *II Timothy 2:3 - 7*.

1)   Soldier in an army. The army is built on discipline. A soldier must always obey his or her commanding officer in everything, otherwise he or she may end up being court-martialled. I believe that some christians need to look at this in relation to their own lives and quit arguing with God who is their commanding officer. Some christians may need to be court-martialled!

If a soldier disobeys his orders in a combat situation, he is likely to be killed or cause others to be killed or come under enemy attack unnecessarily. Many christians are killed or are wounded in battle simply because they are disobedient or undisciplined. Their lack of obedience or discipline may allow satanic attacks on others that could have been avoided. Only God knows the situations and will judge each of us accordingly.

2)   Athlete. When someone cheats in the Olympic games, there is an outcry. If he or she has won a medal he or she is disqualified, and the medal taken away from him or her. The result is tremendous shame and guilt not only on the individual athlete, but also on the country and the organisation that they represent. You can apply this to a spiritual context. See also what Paul teaches us in *I Corinthians 9:24 – 27 ; II Timothy 4:7, 8*.

3)   Farmer. It takes patience and discipline to produce the fruit or crop. It is a tremendous temptation to pick the crop before it is ready for harvest - for example some kids out the back of our place picked watermelons when they were too young - they were ruined and not edible. Think of fruit on a tree - if it is picked too early, it is often hard, and if it does ripen it is often neither sweet nor juicy. This has a spiritual application, which is explained in the next paragraph.

If you give up too early when praying for someone to be converted or to receive the Holy Spirit, the result is that person often becomes ruined spiritually and may become anti-God or anti-religion. To try to grow in the things of God without the proper foundation will end in ruin. Too many christians end up in ruin or are defeated by life and the devil because they try to run before they can walk; or they get involved in intercession or spiritual warfare before they really understand the basics of their christian life.

There are three hindrances to the seed producing the intended crop outlined in the parable of the sower taught by Jesus (*Mark 4:1 - 20*). All of these can be related to discipline.

1)   *Verse 4* Some seeds fell on the path and the birds ate it before it had a chance to grow. The illustration is that some people allow the thoughts of satan, or lust of the flesh, to come and prevent the Word of God producing fruit in their lives. They are undisciplined. As a christian you must learn to recognise these and overcome them in your life.

2)   *Verses 5, 6* Some seed fell in rocky places. There was little soil depth so when trouble came the christian person fell away or gave up. The problem is that there was no deep love relationship with the Lord and no understanding of the deep things of God. There was no detailed study of God's Word or understanding His promises. I believe that if we have his Word hidden in our hearts (by learning memory verses) then we will always know His love and protection and we will not fall away (*Psalm 119:9 - 11*). This requires discipline !

3)   *Verse 7* Some seed fell among weeds or thorns. The deceitfulness of this world and sin will always choke out His Word. It takes discipline to read His Word, pray and come to church meetings when we are enticed to do otherwise. If we are disciplined in our christian life, if we have made up or mind to follow our orders from our supreme commander, then we will never be tempted by the deceitfulness of sin or riches of this world.

       The order of the characteristics of a mature christian life is deliberately chosen by God. Discipline is last. You can have all or most of the others perfect, or nearly perfect, but if you fail on discipline you are likely to be leading yourself and others to ruin. If you want to become the mature christian person God wants you to be, you must be a disciplined christian. The question I need to ask you is this - do you live a disciplined christian life ?

Personal application

This personal application will help you to become a more disciplined person. Answer the following questions honestly before the Lord.

➤ Do I obey my Heavenly Father as my superior officer or try to argue with His commands ?

➤ Have I been in combat situations with the devil and been wounded because I have not been obedient to my orders ?

➤ Do I live my christian life within the rules laid out in God's Word, or do I try and get to the end by cheating ?

➤ Have I the patience to wait for the fruit to mature in my life and in the lives of others or do I attempt to pick it too early ?

➤ Do I have a deep, loving relationship with my Heavenly Father that will last me through the rough times ?

➤ Have I allowed the deceitfulness of sin or the riches of this world to choke out the fruit that God wants to develop in my life ?

➤ Have I allowed my freedom in Christ to become a stumbling block to a brother or sister ?

Make an action plan to try to improve on any you have answered yes to. Implement your action plan and see yourself improve in these areas.

A self-evaluation of what you have learned from this study.

The following personal application is designed to help you evaluate your maturity level as a christian. Are you still a 'babe in Christ' even though you may have been a christian for several or more years ?

The following questions and evaluation scale will help you to rate yourself in all the life qualities we have studied. Circle the number that best represents your self-evaluation, rating from satisfied (1) to dissatisfied (5). It is important that you answer each question honestly for yourself. (No one else needs to see your ratings unless you choose to show them.) If you answer below 3 for every one of them then I believe you are not answering them honestly.

1) How do you assess your reputation as a christian ? Is it above reproach in all areas ?

      Satisfied 1 2 3 4 5 Dissatisfied

2) How do you evaluate your overall relationship with your wife (or husband) ? If you are not married or now divorced or separated, you may skip this question.

      Satisfied 1 2 3 4 5 Dissatisfied

3) Have you or are you developing a biblical perspective for your christian and your overall way of life ?

      Satisfied 1 2 3 4 5 Dissatisfied

4) Do you have a correct view of yourself according to God's Word in relationship to other christians, God, the world, and the people around you ?

      Satisfied 1 2 3 4 5 Dissatisfied

5) Do you live a well-adjusted, respectable life according to the standards of the Word of God ?

      Satisfied 1 2 3 4 5 Dissatisfied

6) Do you use your home to minister to other members of the body of Christ and non-christians ?

      Satisfied 1 2 3 4 5 Dissatisfied

7) Are you able to communicate the Word of God to others in a non-argumentative and non-threating manner ?

      Satisfied 1 2 3 4 5 Dissatisfied

8) Are you addicted to anything that is controlling your life ? Are you doing anything that may cause a weaker christian to stumble and sin against God ?

      Satisfied 1 2 3 4 5 Dissatisfied

9A) Are you known as someone who does not settle your relationship problems with others by violence, either physical, or in actions or words ? Do you refuse to 'push your weight around' or take advantage of someone else because of your position ? Do you allow anger and bitterness to control your feelings towards anyone ?

      Satisfied 1 2 3 4 5 Dissatisfied

9B) Are you mostly a mild-mannered and gentle person, reflecting forgiveness and kindness towards others ?

      Satisfied 1 2 3 4 5 Dissatisfied

10) Are you a peacemaker striving to create harmony and unity, or do you purposely take the opposite point of view from others, stirring up arguments and destroying the unity in the group ?

Satisfied 1 2 3 4 5 Dissatisfied

11) Do you seek first His kingdom and His righteousness more than material possessions or pleasures ? Can you give away material blessings to someone else who needs them more than you do ?

Satisfied 1 2 3 4 5 Dissatisfied

12) Do your spouse and children (if you have any) love and respect you and are they responding to your God and Saviour and His claim on their lives ?

Satisfied 1 2 3 4 5 Dissatisfied

13) Do you boast of what you have accomplished in your christian life, or are you growing in the realisation that without God working through you, you can achieve nothing ?

Satisfied 1 2 3 4 5 Dissatisfied

14) Do you have a good reputation with non-christians ? Do they respect you even though they may disagree with your religious views ?

Satisfied 1 2 3 4 5 Dissatisfied

15) Do you avoid any involvement in questionable activities for a christian, including dishonestly making money ? Do you desire to associate yourself with truth, justice, integrity, and righteousness no matter what the cost ?

Satisfied 1 2 3 4 5 Dissatisfied

16A) Are you satisfied with your level of understanding of the deep truths in God's Word ? Do you encourage others to grow in sound doctrine ?

Satisfied 1 2 3 4 5 Dissatisfied

16B) Can you gently refute others who refuse to listen to the truth of God's Word without becoming argumentative ?

Satisfied 1 2 3 4 5 Dissatisfied

17) Do you seek to have your own way in church leadership or other meetings and are you a team player ?

Satisfied 1 2 3 4 5 Dissatisfied

18) Do you actively strive to do good to others in all situations and avoid all appearances of evil ?

Satisfied 1 2 3 4 5 Dissatisfied

19) Are you able to make objective decisions and be honest in your relationships with other people ? Do you strive to obey the law, including traffic laws and your dealings with the tax office or Centrelink ?

Satisfied 1 2 3 4 5 Dissatisfied

20) Are you actively pursuing after personal and practical holiness ?

Satisfied 1 2 3 4 5 Dissatisfied

21) Are you in the process of continual growth in your christian life, becoming more and more like Jesus Christ ? Do you have a disciplined prayer life and personal bible study ?

Satisfied 1 2 3 4 5 Dissatisfied

Now go back and check those items that you circled that have the highest numbers. Set up a priority list for personal action.

Implement this list over the coming weeks and months – in other words do something positive to improve the life qualities you are weakest in and rejoice with God over the progress you have made.

Make a date in your diary or planner to revisit your personal action plan and undertake this self-evaluation every 6 months.

Be encouraged as you make progress towards growing into a mature christian that God desires you to be.

References

Jay P. Green (1976) "*The New Englishmen's Greek Concordance*", Copyright 1976 by Jay P. Green, Published by Associated Publishers and Authors, Inc, Lafayette, Indiana, USA.

Guthrie, D., Motyer, J.A., Stibbs, A.M. and Wiseman, D.J. (1976) "*The New Bible Commentary Revised*", Third edition. Copyright Inter-Varsity Press, Leicester, England, revised and reprinted 1976.

Joseph Henry Thayer (1979) "*The New Thayer's Greek-English Lexicon of the New Testament*", Lafayette, Indiana, USA, Copyright Christian Copyrights, Inc

"*The Exhaustive Concordance of The Bible by James Strong*" (referenced as 'Strong's Concordance' in this book) quoted from the website *biblehub. com/strongs.htm*. Accessed at various times during 2021 calendar year.

The Lockman Foundation (1981) "*New American Standard Exhaustive Concordance of the Bible, Hebrew-Aramaic and Greek Dictionaries*", Robert L. Thomas, General Editor, Published by Holman, Nashville, Tennessee, USA, Copyright The Lockman Foundation 1981.

"*Barnes Notes on the Bible*" quoted from the website *biblehub.com/ commentaries/barnes.htm* Accessed at various times during 2021 calendar year.

"*Matthew Henry's Commentary on the whole Bible*" (referenced as '*Matthew Henry's commentary*' in this book) quoted from the website *biblehub.com/ mhcw.htm*. Accessed at various times during 2021 calendar year.

Other books by the same author

Ten lessons on spiritual leadership from the life of Elijah (in preparation)

Lessons from the Kings of Israel and Judah (in preparation)

What can we learn from the Lord's Prayer ? (in preparation)

www.ingramcontent.com/pod-product-compliance
Lightning Source LLC
Chambersburg PA
CBHW011802090426
42811CB00044B/2455/J